TOUCHPEBBLES
VOLUME A - TEACHER'S GUIDE

Herndon Elementary School
630 Dranesville Road
Herndon, VA 20170

Published by

TOUCHSTONES
DISCUSSION PROJECT

About the Touchstones Discussion Project

The Touchstones Discussion Project is a nonprofit organization founded on the belief that all people can benefit from the listening, speaking, thinking, and interpersonal skills gained by engaging in active, focused discussions. Since 1984, Touchstones has helped millions of students and others develop and improve these skills in school, work, and life. For more information about the Touchstones Discussion Project, visit www.touchstones.org.

Texts selected, translated, and edited by
Geoffrey Comber
Howard Zeiderman
Nick Maistrellis

©1993, 2003
by Touchstones Discussion Project
522 Chesapeake Avenue
Annapolis, Maryland 21403
800-456-6542
www.touchstones.org

All rights reserved. No part of this book,
except worksheets for classroom use,
may be reproduced in any form
without prior consent of the authors.

ISBN 1-878461-64-8

Acknowledgments

We would like to thank the following for their help in the publication of this volume:

Hound and Hunter, by Winslow Homer, 1892, oil on canvas. Gift of Stephen C. Clack, copyright 1994 Board of Trustees, National Gallery of Art, Washington, DC.

Portrait of a Clergyman, by Albrecht Dürer, 1516, oil on parchment, Samuel H. Kress Collection, copyright 1994 Board of Trustees, National Gallery of Art, Washington, DC.

Marchesa Brigida Spinola Doria, by Peter Paul Rubens, 1606, oil canvas. Samuel H. Kress Collection, copyright 1994 Board of Trustees, National Gallery of Art, Washington, DC.

The Much Resounding Sea, by Thomas Moran, 1884, oil on canvas. Gift of the Avakon Foundation, copyright 1994 Board of Trustees, National Gallery of Art, Washington, DC.

Waves at Matsushima, detail from a six-fold screen, by Sotatsu, seventeenth century, color and gold on paper. Freer Gallery of Art, Smithsonian Institution, Washington, DC.: Gift of Charles Lang Freer, F1906.232.

The illustrations on pages 28, 36, 41, 49, 65, 72, 79, 101, 109, 121, 156, 164, 170, 192, 196, 205, and 222 were provided by Shirley Stickney.

The illustrations on pages 87, 92, 175, 185, and 212 were provided by Anna Lord.

The illustrations on pages 134 and 141 were provided by John Norton.

Contents

Introduction 1

The Touchpebbles Text 5

Leading a Touchpebbles Discussion 9

Skills Your Students Will Build 13

Touchpebbles: How to Prepare and What to Expect 19

1. A Different Kind of Class 23

2. The Judge
   A Tale from West Africa 31

3. The Camel and the Jackal
   A Tale from India 37

4. The Clever Thief
   A Tale from Korea 43

5. Hound and Hunter
   by Winslow Homer 53

6. The Lion and the Mouse
   by Aesop 59

7. A Test of Strength
   A Tale of the Fan Tribe of Africa 67

8. Pandora's Box
   A Tale from Greece 75

9. The Confessions
   by Saint Augustine of Hippo 81

10. Emile or On Education
    by Jean Jacques Rousseau 89

11. The Pillow
    A Tale from the Middle East 95

12. Catching Fish in the Forest
    A Tale from Russia 103

13. The Eagle
    by Alfred, Lord Tennyson 111

14. They Share the Work
    A Tale from Latvia 117

15. Two Portraits:
    Portrait of a Clergyman, *by Albrecht Dürer*
    Marchesa Brigida Spinola Doria, *by Peter Paul Rubens* 123

16. The Republic
    by Plato 131

17. How to Catch a Thief
    A Tale from China 137

18. Definitions of a Straight Line 143

19. Gilgamesh the King
    An Epic from Ancient Persia 151

20. The Weapons of King Chuko
    by Lo Kuan Chung 159

21. The Odyssey
    by Homer 165

22. How Much Is a Son Worth?
    A Tale from Saudi Arabia 171

23. Images of Waves:
    The Much Resounding Sea, *by Thomas Moran*
    Waves at Matsushima, *by Sotatsu* 177

24. About Lying
    by Michel de Montaigne 181

25. The Man Who Thought He Could Do Anything
    A Tale of the Algonquin People. 187

26. Robinson Crusoe
    by Daniel Defoe 193

27. Narcissus
    A Story from Greece 201

28. The Spider and the Turtle
    A Tale of the Ashanti People of Africa 207

29. Map of Iceland
    from the cover of Touchpebbles Volume A. 213

30. The Histories
    by Herodotus 219

APPENDICES 225

Introduction

As the world changes, so must the ways we teach and learn. Our world is becoming more interconnected, bringing together people with diverse backgrounds and different perspectives. Technology places volumes of information at our fingertips. Skills such as problem-solving in groups, processing and evaluating new information, and working with diverse groups of people are more important than ever to students' success. Now, students must also learn how to teach themselves.

Touchstones Empowers Students

The Touchstones Discussion Project offers students and teachers the tools to meet the demands of their emerging environment. Students of all backgrounds and skill levels—across the United States and around the world—currently participate in Touchstones classes. In their weekly Touchstones Discussions, students learn strategies to help them navigate through school and through life. Touchstones helps students learn to process information, ask meaningful questions, and enlist the help of others in making decisions. As students listen, explore, cooperate, and solve problems, they become collaborators in their own learning. They learn that life is not always about right or wrong answers but often about better or worse decisions.

Touchstones Empowers Teachers

Not only do students learn how to learn, teachers learn a new way to teach. The Touchstones Discussion Method offers teachers a powerful new approach to group discussion that results in full, active, and eager participation by their students. Eventually, the students themselves take the lead in the process. By connecting students' schoolwork with their experiences outside school, Touchstones Discussions bring the classroom to life.

THE TOUCHSTONES DISCUSSION METHOD

Although most people can join a group conversation and be polite and not interrupt, the development of higher-level discussion skills requires time, practice, and guidance. Carefully chosen texts, an effective discussion leader, and basic discussion ground rules are essential in a Touchstones Discussion. As students progress through the lessons in this Touchpebbles volume, they will have the opportunity to acquire fundamental listening, speaking, and thinking skills, and they will become better learners, capable of teaching themselves and others.

Touchstones develops these skills through the systematic use of individual work, small group work, and large group discussion—all grounded in texts that exercise specific skills and highlight the discussion process itself. Touchstones does indeed teach students how to participate in discussions. But most importantly, Touchstones helps students hone the skills that will increase their abilities to gain from their entire education.

What Is a Touchstones Discussion?

A discussion is a cooperative exploration of ideas, in which all participants have an equal right to speak and learn and an equal responsibility to listen and make room for others. Touchstones Discussions offer a setting in which students, by sharing and examining their ideas, can come to a greater understanding of themselves and others.

A discussion is not a debate, a casual conversation, a question-and-answer session, or a simple sharing of stories. A discussion has no rigid agenda and no goal of reaching a definite conclusion.

THE TOUCHPEBBLES SERIES

Touchpebbles is the Touchstones program specifically designed for use in grades three through five. The texts used in Touchpebbles are appropriate for younger students, and the activities students engage in are more concrete and specific than those in Touchstones' programs for older students. However, the framework of the Touchpebbles series is essentially the same as that of all Touchstones programs. In Touchpebbles, students are asked to complete a partially finished painting, to propose plausible solutions to problems, to consider multiple perspectives, and to rewrite stories, comparing their own versions with those of the author. By asking students to engage in imaginative manipulation, construction, and open-ended discussion, Touchpebbles involves students in their education, helps them take the initiative in the classroom, and fosters their sense of responsibility for their learning.

YOUR TOUCHPEBBLES CLASS

Every Touchpebbles class has the same basic structure. Your students do not prepare prior to class (student volumes are kept in the classroom). You and your students sit in a circle. The circular seating arrangement, as opposed to rows or a horseshoe configuration, encourages your students to speak to one another and not through you.

The short Touchpebbles Text is read twice: first, you read it aloud while students read along silently. Reading it aloud allows students of all reading levels to participate. Then your students silently read it again. Next, you usually give your students a few minutes to work individually on their worksheets, which pose a few questions about issues addressed in the text. Once the worksheets have been completed, your students broaden their perspectives by working together in small groups or pairs, either by comparing their worksheet answers or by completing a collaborative task. Finally, the entire class returns to the large circle for the large group discussion.

> **CLASS OVERVIEW**
> - The students do not prepare.
> - The whole class, including the teacher, sits in a circle.
> - The teacher reads the Touchpebbles Text aloud. The students read the text silently.
> - The students do individual work.
> - The students do small group work.
> - The teacher asks an open-ended question to start the discussion.
> - The students do not raise hands.
> - All participants follow the ground rules.

Begin the large group discussion by asking a brief, open-ended question about a topic raised in the text. Your students should speak to the group (not to you) without raising their hands. The discussion ends without closure, thus encouraging your students to continue thinking about the topics that have been raised in the class.

Students follow the Touchpebbles ground rules (see the box) throughout the lesson. These simple ground rules establish a framework within which genuine discussion can take place. With no rules, the discussion would differ little from a conversation with friends, and the academic aspects and seriousness of the activity would thus be lost.

> **TOUCHPEBBLES GROUND RULES**
> 1. We do not raise our hands when we want to speak.
> 2. We speak to everyone in the class and not just to our neighbors and friends.
> 3. We do not interrupt when others are speaking.
> 4. We listen carefully to what other students say.

The Touchpebbles Text

The Touchstones staff chooses texts that spark discussions and develop skills. Thus the texts in this Touchpebbles volume are an inseparable part of the Touchstones Discussion Method. The texts are arranged in a sequence that fosters the students' skills development.

For example, the texts used early in the Touchpebbles curriculum are particularly helpful in exploring the issues that arise when students form discussion groups for the first time. These texts feature the kinds of topics—life changes, friendship, revenge, and wealth—that can easily be related to the students' experiences and can facilitate the sharing of ideas. Making discussions accessible moves the group toward the early goal of high participation rates. Furthermore, in the discussion of these texts, your students are developing such critical reading skills as the ability to integrate their experience with the ideas put forth in the text. Later in the volume, your students will grapple with denser, more challenging texts—including excerpts from philosophical, scientific, or mathematical works—that encourage them to work together to understand the meaning of the text. Such cooperative textual analysis is made possible by the earlier process of group formation, and it builds on the critical reading skills already developed.

Although the order of the Touchpebbles Texts is designed to lead to specific outcomes, the texts are so rich and multifaceted that each can be useful for generating a variety of outcomes. You, as the Touchpebbles Discussion leader, can use the text, as well as your opening and follow-up

A TOUCHSTONES TEXT:
- Reveals students' thoughts and opinions.
- Encourages certain discussion dynamics and skills.
- Is short and requires no preparation.
- May be drawn from any of various sources: classics from Western and other civilizations, folktales, modern works, and reproductions of visual arts.
- Unites the familiar and unfamiliar, the well-known and the strange.

questions, to achieve the goals you have set for the class. For example, if you have decided to work toward greater student participation, then you could use questions that directly invite students to share their experience. However, if students who excel in traditional class formats have been silent in, and removed from, the Touchpebbles Discussions, you might use questions that are directly related to the text to help those students feel comfortable enough to contribute to the discussion.

> **WHAT IS A TOUCHSTONE?**
> A touchstone was a stone used by jewelers to determine the quality of gold or silver. The metal to be tested was scratched on a smooth black stone, and the scratch-mark indicated the purity of the metal. The touchstone was a tool used to reveal the nature of another thing.
> Texts serve as the touchstone in a Touchstones Discussion class by revealing the thoughts, hidden talents, abilities, and expectations of the group members. Just as a touchstone was not itself precious but was an important tool, so too the Touchstones Text is not itself the reason for the discussion but is an essential tool for it.

TEXTS AS TOUCHSTONES

Clearly, the role of texts in Touchpebbles Discussions differs greatly from the role of texts in regular classes. The Touchpebbles Texts serve primarily as skill-building tools, or touchstones (see the box). Although the content of the text is important, the mastery of subject matter is not a goal of this class. In Touchpebbles, your students develop skills for mastering the content in their other classes.

Touchpebbles Texts Are Short and Thought Provoking

To serve as touchstones, the texts are short—rarely more than one and one-half pages long—and they can be discussed without preparation. Short texts give all the students equal access to the learning experience regardless of their abilities and willingness to do work outside class. The brevity and simplicity of the texts facilitate discussion and reduce the reliance on one-way summary and explanation (given by you or by well-prepared students). Furthermore, a short text enables your students to keep in mind a sense of the text as a whole as they discuss it. These text characteristics set Touchstones apart from other discussion programs.

Touchpebbles Texts Stand Alone

Because these texts are serving as touchstones and not as content to be mastered, no background information is needed. Supplying such information generally runs counter to the goal of genuine discussion. For instance, if you display information about the author or the context of the passage, then your students will continue to look to you to explain the text instead of learning to actively work with the text as a group. Furthermore, background information puts the focus on the content of the text, whereas the Touchpebbles Discussion should be focused on the thoughts and opinions of the students. As your students develop skills and become better able to hold a discussion, they might attend closely to the text at times, which is fine as long as the goal remains to have a true discussion that clarifies students' own thoughts and opinions.

Touchpebbles Texts Blend the Familiar and the Strange

One characteristic that is shared by all the texts is that they combine the familiar and the unfamiliar, the well-known and the strange—which is another reason they should be used without background information. Each text is familiar because it involves a concept, attitude, or issue with which everyone has had experience. A text might raise questions about competition or making decisions, for example, or it might address the differences between science and art. Familiarity with the topic is important for the discussion because it allows all your students to contribute on the basis of their experiences. All students should feel equally capable of discussing the text.

Most Touchpebbles Texts are drawn from a distant time or a foreign culture and are in some way strange: the author might address a familiar concern in a surprising way or have a viewpoint that is not clear. The strangeness encourages students to work cooperatively to understand the message of the texts. Also, facing the unfamiliar allows students to distance themselves from their own assumptions and better discern their true thoughts. The strange aspects of the texts should not be explained away with background information. For instance, attributing the opinions in a text to the author's era and society might encourage students to think of the differences as merely cultural phenomena and prevent them from seriously trying to understand and explore unusual perspectives. Touchpebbles Texts are not about current events or hot topics because such readings would tend to reinforce the opinions of some participants and run counter to the opinions of others. The result would be speech-making or argument rather than discussion.

The combination of the familiar and the strange affects the preparation as well as the selection of the Touchpebbles Texts. Texts not originally written in English have been newly translated, and all texts have been edited so that the language is appropriate for the reading level. However, the complexity of the opinions and ideas in the texts has been preserved. Your students may find some texts quite challenging; such difficult work is well suited to cooperative efforts.

The texts derive from the vast richness of human experience; they deal with such issues as power, control, fear, revenge, friendship, love, and beauty. The scope, familiarity and strangeness, skill-specific aspects, and brevity of the texts make them effective as touchstones for a discussion. The texts are always carefully chosen to serve as touchstones for meaningful discussions in which students, while gaining skills, are learning about fundamental principles, discovering the roles of these principles in the world around them, and reflecting on their own thoughts and actions.

Leading a Touchpebbles Discussion

YOUR ROLE AS THE DISCUSSION LEADER

As a Touchpebbles Discussion leader, you must carefully guide your students through their individual work, small group work, and large group discussions in a way that allows them to take as much ownership of the process as possible. Before each Touchpebbles class, you will need to prepare by deciding on strategies that address the needs of your group. Reviewing the problems or successes in past discussions will help you set appropriate objectives for each session. These objectives, in turn, will give you insights into the type of opening question that you should use, what to look for in the small group work, or a skill or behavior that you need to model for your students. This preparation will also enable you to adjust quickly and respond appropriately to unanticipated issues or events because you will have a larger goal in mind. Because different skills are developed at different stages of a discussion group's history, continually reviewing the group's progress is a part of your role as discussion leader.

During the class, your tasks are to assist students by clarifying the worksheet exercises, encourage exploration and cooperative discussion, monitor the ways in which your students are practicing particular skills, and employ various interventions that facilitate discussion. Although you will not be imparting information or communicating facts to students, you will be continually active. Each of the discussion class's three parts (individual work, small group or pair work, and large group discussion) requires a different type of leadership.

Your Role in Individual Work

In both individual and small group activities, you will act very much as you do in a content-area class. In the individual work, students might have questions or might not understand some parts of the worksheets, and disciplinary problems might arise because students are in a different seating arrangement. Manage these situations as you normally would. Move around the room to assist or monitor your students during this part of the class.

Each lesson includes a student worksheet featuring questions related to the text. Sometimes the text is read before the students work on the worksheet, sometimes after. Whatever the sequence, the leader reads both the text and the worksheet aloud to the students. You should not ask students to be the public readers, because not all of them will be able to read equally well and preferences may be established, which would run counter to the skills-development process in Touchpebbles. Once your students begin working on the worksheet, be available when they need assistance but do not be overly active except in disciplinary matters.

Your Role in Small Group and Pair Work

Your level of activity will be greater in small group work than in individual work. After reading aloud the directions on the worksheet, divide the students into groups. However you select the groups, make sure that they are mixed regularly, and that within the groups, certain students do not always take the same roles. Spend some time with each group. The small group work usually involves students' trying to reach a consensus on some question, although in many cases they will not be able to do so. Coming to a consensus is not as important as making the attempt. The attempt involves listening to the opinions of others, presenting views, and articulating points of difference. Keep these goals in mind while you help your students stay on task and articulate the problems that they face.

Your Role in Large Group Discussions

Leading the large group discussions is the most demanding and multifaceted aspect of running Touchpebbles classes. To foster the skills development that occurs during cooperative inquiry, you will need to monitor the content and dynamics of the discussion and make decisions accordingly. You will need to help your students learn how to relate the text to their experience and prior knowledge. And all the while, you must work toward the goal of having your students share these responsibilities with you. Over time, you will learn new skills and new ways to use your personal teaching strengths in this new context.

The Conscience of the Group. The discussion leader is often described as being the "conscience of the group." During the large group discussion, the leader's role is to create and maintain the conditions under which students can freely explore ideas and have a cooperative discussion. You should always be considering the content and dynamics of the discussion and the development of skills. Pay attention to what the students are talking about, how they are interacting as a group, and what skills they must practice to become better participants and eventually share the responsibility for conducting the discussion. You must constantly be making decisions about whether or how to intervene in the discussion. Successful discussions will not occur without your continual attention and monitoring. From beginning to end, discussion leaders attend to the group's needs by, for instance, drawing out a shy student or getting students who dislike each other to collaborate. Leaders should look for successes and possibilities and decide on possible interventions, such as asking follow-up questions or creating a rotating system of discussion observers.

Relating Text and Experience. In your role, one of the most important general principles to remember is that the text is not to be mastered. Faced with an interesting text, you might be tempted to highlight intriguing or essential passages and ask highly textual questions. But in doing so, you would be teaching about the text instead of leading the discussion. Keep in mind that Touchpebbles classes should always focus on the interplay between the text and the students' experiences and opinions. Only in this way will the students take responsibility for the course of the discussion and develop their intellectual curiosity. With your help, they will eventually make the discussions more text-oriented. At times, your students will not refer to the text for long periods of time, especially in the group's first few discussions. Although you might decide to ask questions that refer to the text, you should not hold the students to the text. Doing so would play to the strengths of a few students while disregarding those of others. Later in the volume, the students should be freely relating the text and their own opinions and ideas. As such skills as exploring various perspectives and recognizing assumptions come more into play, have the students explore and address the text, but no more than they explore and address one another's ideas.

Sharing Responsibility. The students need to share with you the responsibility for the discussions. During the first discussions, you, as the conscience of the group, will have the greatest responsibility for the dynamics and content of the discussions. However, an important part of the skills development in Touchpebbles comes from students' solving problems and addressing group-dynamics issues. As the class progresses through the volume, the students must assume more responsibility for the discussion's success. For this reason, you might occasionally want to let problems occur and allow the students the opportunity to correct them.

A common problem in the first few discussions is that many students speak at once. Because speaking in class without raising their hands is a new experience for students, you should expect situations in your discussions in which three, four, or more students are speaking simultaneously. Such a stiuation is the type of circumstance that might require intervention.

First, keep in mind that discussion skills are difficult to develop and are best gained when students recognize what actions are needed when a problem arises. You should not always avoid problems that make obvious the need for, and utility of, certain skills. These skills include anticipating the direction of a discussion, being aware of who is beginning or trying to speak, and keeping in mind the importance of both speaking and allowing others to speak.

If many students are speaking at the same time, you might allow the situation to continue for a short time, perhaps ten seconds. Allow the students to observe that the discussion has broken down. After a short time, intervene if the group has not corrected the problem. You might point out that it is impossible to understand anyone with so many people speaking at one time. You might then ask the students to repeat what they were saying or even call on them successively—but do not employ hand raising. You will have let them experience the problem and will have given them a short-term solution. The goal will then be for your students to identify the problem when it recurs and to correct it themselves.

If you find that this particular problem reappears frequently, use a different approach. When the problem occurs and has not been corrected, stop the discussion, describe the problem, and ask the class to decide how to solve it. If some students do not see talking simultaneously as a problem, you should permit others to explain why it is a problem and what effect it has on them and the group. When you allow the students to suggest ways to avoid this problem, some may want to introduce hand raising or some other form of taking turns that is mediated by the teacher. If so, explain the goals of Touchpebbles and why this type of solution would hinder the development of several discussion skills.

Touchpebbles and Your Other Classes. Although the approach in Touchpebbles classes differs from that in such content classes as science, English, social studies, and mathematics, both approaches are essential—and even complementary—in any sound educational environment. Touchpebbles gives students tools with which to master the subjects in their content classes by helping them learn to work cooperatively, solve problems, and think analytically and creatively. In turn, content classes supply a pool of information and skills that students can bring to a Touchpebbles Discussion. Such knowledge broadens the discussion by enabling students to see connections within the curriculum and also between schoolwork and the world outside school.

As you begin to lead Touchpebbles Discussions, remember that leading discussions is a skill that you will learn just as you have learned many others. Any teacher who conducts a content class proficiently can also learn to lead Touchpebbles Discussions. You are not expected to surrender the individual teaching strengths that already serve you well. Instead, you will learn how to employ these strengths in a new context and toward different goals. In the large group discussion, you will learn to notice the occasions that require a decision and possible intervention. Whether and how you intervene will be determined by how you have adapted your teaching strengths to the goals of the Touchstones Discussion Project.

Skills Your Students Will Build

STUDENT OUTCOMES

The Touchstones Discussion Method cultivates students' academic and social skills. Many students who don't excel in other learning environments thrive in their Touchpebbles class. For some students, Touchpebbles brings a new sense of relevance to their education. Some gain respect for others and learn to work with them regardless of their social or academic backgrounds. Although Touchpebbles Discussions offer different benefits for different students, all students benefit from better critical thinking, reading, speaking, and listening skills while becoming more actively involved in their education.

Students Develop Critical Thinking and Reading Skills

Critical thinking skills are exercised in all aspects of Touchpebbles Discussions throughout the year. Individually and in small and large groups, students evaluate opinions, generate ideas, and identify important facets of the topic being discussed. Because students are asked to consider difficult and unfamiliar questions that do not have clear right and wrong answers, they practice creative problem-solving, making inferences, and inductive as well as deductive reasoning. They become more confident and competent when making decisions amid great uncertainty.

Although the purpose of a Touchpebbles Discussion is not students' mastery of the text, the discussion of the topics presented in the text helps students develop important reading strategies and

CRITICAL THINKING SKILLS
- Identifying important issues
- Confronting difficult questions
- Evaluating opinions and evidence
- Generating ideas
- Making inferences
- Recognizing assumptions

CRITICAL READING SKILLS
- Relating a text to experience
- Using questioning strategies
- Analyzing a text
- Supporting opinions with evidence in a text
- Asking critical questions
- Exploring various interpretations

abilities that will make them critical readers. Such readers ask critical questions, compare their own ideas with those in the text, make textual inferences, use the text to challenge or support ideas, and apply their previous knowledge and experience; all these skills play an important role in Touchpebbles Discussions. These skills help students become better readers by offering them different avenues for understanding the text—from a general understanding of what is being discussed to the personal understanding gained from relating their experiences to the topic at hand. To determine an author's assumptions and point of view, students must first make their own points of view explicit. To draw inferences requires the ability to evaluate evidence. For each of these skills to develop, students must learn how to look at themselves so that they can identify and understand the assumptions that have shaped their thoughts and opinions. Achieving such important personal distance requires the assistance and cooperation of others that occurs in the Touchstones Discussion format.

Students Develop Discussion Skills

The discussion and cooperation skills at the foundation of the Touchstones Discussion Method reinforce and refine critical thinking and critical reading abilities. Because the discussion questions do not have definitive answers and the texts are unfamiliar, students realize that they need to work together to understand complex ideas and make decisions. Furthermore, because individual students have strengths and weaknesses (some typical examples are described in the chart below), they learn to look to others for help in overcoming their weaknesses and

STRENGTHS AND WEAKNESSES OF STUDENTS IN DISCUSSION

STRENGTH	WEAKNESS
Student A	
• Follows teacher's lead	• Expects teacher's approval
• Attends to text	• Does not speak or listen to classmates
• Gives clear and precise answers	• Is uncomfortable with uncertainty
Student B	
• Acts independently of teacher	• May exhibit antagonistic behavior
• Thinks about serious issues in terms of personal experience	• Finds no place in school for the seriousness with which he or she considers life
• Is not afraid of being wrong	• Does not know how to receive criticism
Student C	
• Listens equally to teacher and student	• Does not take initiative in classroom
• Follows topic of discussion	• Does not initiate new lines of inquiry
• Acts as member of group	• Does not take individual responsibility for actions and opinions

similarly to offer their strengths to help others overcome their limitations. Recognizing others' strengths and knowing how to learn from others are important skills developed in Touchpebbles classes. For example, a student who reads closely needs the student who listens very well; a student who excels at making decisions in clear-cut situations with right and wrong answers needs the student who can see the big picture and isn't afraid to take chances; the analytical student needs the creative thinker—and vice versa.

At different stages of a discussion group's progress, different skills are developed and practiced. During the initial discussions, students are asked to share their responses to a text as well as their experiences and opinions. From that point, group formation begins. Soliciting students' experiences—the one thing about which they are all experts—makes all students equally capable of contributing. During the early discussions, participation increases and quieter students find their way into the conversation. The experiences that your students are asked to share are those that relate to the topic covered by the text. This is the first step toward integrating past experience and prior knowledge with the subject of the text or the topic at hand. Such skill at integrating experience and knowledge extends beyond the Touchpebbles Discussion into all areas of study.

> **DISCUSSION SKILLS**
> - Cooperating with all classmates
> - Stating ideas clearly
> - Exploring various perspectives
> - Following lines of discussion and thought
> - Relating directly to peers
> - Analyzing group effectiveness
> - Reflecting on viewpoint of self and others
> - Respecting others' opinions
> - Asking questions to clarify the discussion
> - Formulating complex ideas

As the collection of individuals coalesces into a whole group, students begin to gain a sense of ownership of the process—they view it as an academic activity that belongs to them, and they understand that they share the responsibility for its success. They become more concerned with being understood and recognize the value of speaking clearly and rephrasing their statements. Over time, students devise strategies for speaking to different audiences and become better at forming complex ideas.

As students assume ownership of the discussion process, they become more willing to ask questions when they do not understand—another skill that transfers to their other classes. They also begin speaking directly to one another and not just through you as the discussion leader. This student-to-student interaction is an early indicator that students are beginning to think of their classmates as people from whom they can learn. Without this sense of respect and value, no cooperative learning can occur.

Because they cannot all talk at once and are specifically reminded by the ground rules (discussed on page 3) not to interrupt, students learn both how to find opportunities to speak and how to allow others to speak. Students are also introduced, indirectly, to the different ways each one thinks and learns and the variety of experiences that shape their opinions and their perspectives. This personal understanding is even more essential in the small group activities in which they are asked to move beyond their individual considerations to make group decisions or come to a group consensus. The small and large group exercises help students learn the skills necessary for working with others, from respecting others and exploring various perspectives to supporting ideas with evidence and reflecting on their own views and assumptions.

Small group work also fosters cooperation skills by encouraging collaboration among students who might not otherwise work together. In any discussion group, subgroups will emerge. Often these groupings are based on preexisting relationships; for example, friends or teammates may form a subgroup. Students gravitate to those with whom they have something academically or socially in common and might initially be willing to work only with those friends. This tendency must be overcome by the group. Touchpebbles gives you lessons and tools to help your students learn the value of new perspectives and recognize that they have fundamental commonalities with all their classmates.

Students Become Active Listeners

Active listening is probably the most challenging communication skill to develop. To be active listeners, students must listen to all members of the group, be willing to accept what is different, and be aware of the presuppositions and habits of thinking that can prevent them from understanding what others are saying. Active listening includes both listening carefully and trying to understand other people on their own terms.

In Touchpebbles classes, active-listening skills are developed through the text and the other members of the group. The first step is having students examine their response to the text, which speaks to something familiar in an unfamiliar way. By considering and exploring the differences between the author's thinking and their own, students begin to recognize their similarities. They realize that they share a world with one another that they do not share with the author. In this way, discussions help clarify their world picture. When students listen carefully, they recognize that, although they share a world, they have traveled different paths through this world. Thus the importance of listening carefully to one another is understood and valued. Certain Touchpebbles lessons also help students explore their listening weaknesses and strengths—for example, that they sometimes do not listen because their opinion differs from that

ACTIVE LISTENING SKILLS
- Focusing attention on the speaker
- Listening respectfully
- Understanding and accepting different opinions
- Identifying preconceptions that inhibit listening
- Asking questions that clarify points and promote discussion

of the speaker or that different purposes and goals keep them from listening. Students learn that they must be prepared to listen to views they do not expect to hear and that they must make room for speakers to say what they wish to say in their own terms.

Students Collaborate in Their Education

All too often, school experiences lead students to believe that they are expected to be passive. This circumstance is counterproductive on two counts. First, the emerging independence of your students is not capitalized on but resisted. And second, the long-range goal for students—that they cease being merely students and become able to teach themselves—is not fully incorporated into their educational experience. In addition to developing critical thinking and discussion skills, Touchpebbles effects a major change in students—they begin to cooperate actively in their education.

Weekly Touchpebbles classes create an academic environment in which students determine the content of the discussion. Their experiences, opinions, desires, fears, and uncertainties bring to life the ideas raised in the texts. Their interests and questions determine the avenues the discussion will take. Students eventually realize the need to collaborate with one another to make the discussion successful. They learn to contribute their respective strengths and assist one another in compensating for and correcting their respective weaknesses. In addition, they begin to desire to collaborate with the teachers and students in other classes because they see the value of collaboration and have learned how to take the initiative in the classroom. Although discussions will not and should not be the principal method of teaching content, Touchpebbles Discussions create the expectation that students will learn how to teach themselves. To meet this expectation, students and teachers alike must assume new responsibilities and develop new skills.

Touchpebbles: How to Prepare and What to Expect

CONTENTS

Conducting weekly Touchstones Discussions with the Touchpebbles curriculum is a challenging and rewarding experience. The *Touchpebbles Teacher's Guide* gives you the tools to help make your discussions substantive and successful. The *Teacher's Guide* includes thirty lessons that are carefully planned around selected Touchpebbles readings. Each lesson is designed for a forty-minute class, but if your actual class time is longer or shorter, feel free to modify the times allocated for the activities in the lesson.

You will find the following in each lesson.

1. **Icons.** The icons have two roles. The icons on the first page of each lesson, ordered from left to right, give you a snapshot of the activities in the lesson and the order in which the activities take place. The icons found elsewhere in the volume help you find particular sections of each lesson quickly and easily.

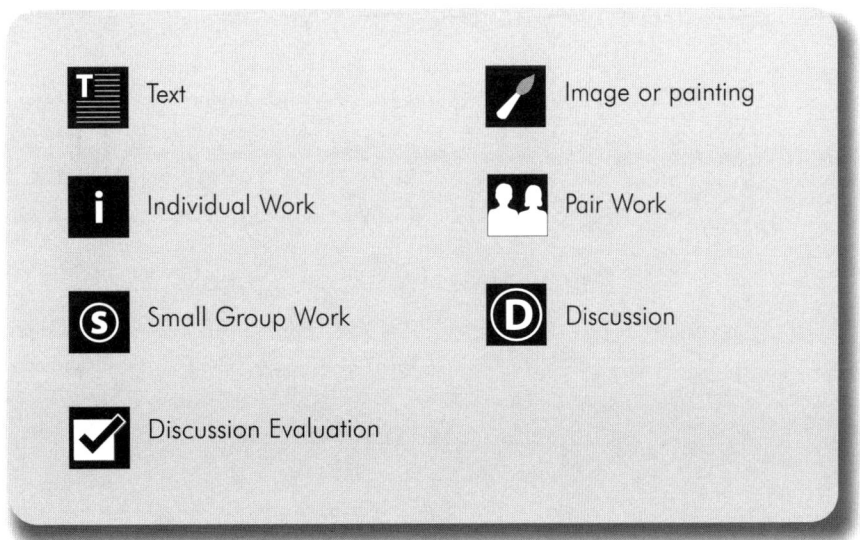

2. **Purpose.** In each lesson you will find descriptions of the broad goals that Touchpebbles aims to achieve over time as well as the specific objectives that you are to reach in the lesson.

3. **Introduction.** A brief introduction highlights the central themes and ideas of the lesson.

4. **Lesson Summary.** This section briefly summarizes the text and its connection to the individual and small group activities.

5. **Possible Questions to Raise.** Any or all of the suggested questions can be used during the large group discussion, although you should feel free to create your own questions. Always keep in mind that the questions may need to be rephrased for your particular group of students.

6. **Lesson Plan.** The lesson plan allows you to see at a glance the day's activities and the approximate amount of time you should take for each part of the lesson.

7. **The Text.** The complete text, as it appears in the student volumes, is included in your *Teacher's Guide* so that you will have the same material right at your fingertips.

8. **The Worksheet.** The individual and small group activities appear on the worksheet. Please be certain to make enough copies of the worksheet for each student to have one.

ADDITIONAL FEATURES

To help you monitor students' progress and know approximately when certain signs of progress should appear, the *Teacher's Guide* contains **benchmarks** at appropriate junctures in the volume. These nine benchmarks serve as a skills map, indicating when you should expect to see certain improvements among the students in your group.

Periodic **evaluations** of your discussion group's strengths and weaknesses will give you the information you need to set goals and measure progress. This *Teacher's Guide* includes seven group evaluation sheets—one appearing at the end of every three or four lessons. Each one briefly describes how to use the evaluation, given the particular stage of your group, and includes four to eight questions for you—not your students—to complete.

PREPARING FOR THE LESSON

As a Touchpebbles Discussion leader, your preparation is the key to guiding your students through a successful lesson. Allow about one hour for this preparation at first, then increase or decrease the time as needed. High-quality preparation includes the following steps:

1. Read the entire lesson.
2. Read the text several times, marking the parts that interest you.

3. Reflect on previous discussions.
4. Determine a goal for your group.
5. Choose or create opening and follow-up questions.
6. Make sure you have the required materials (copies of the worksheet and any materials required for the individual and small group activities).

EXPECTATIONS

As you begin your Touchpebbles program, be ready with a few expectations about the challenges and rewards of the process. You and your students may experience some initial discomfort with the Touchstones Discussion Method. Speaking directly to one another without raising their hands first is likely to be a new experience for many students, and it will take time for them to feel comfortable with the new procedures. Keep in mind that helping students become comfortable in this new situation is an integral part of the process. You will need to let them experiment with this new situation if they are to learn how to accomodate one another without your constant mediation.

You too may feel a little uncomfortable in this new setting. Teachers often feel as if they have relinquished control of their classroom during the discussion. Remember that even though you are no longer the authority on the text, you are still the authority in the class.

You should also expect to see great progress from your students in Touchpebbles. They will soon move past their unease and begin taking ownership of the discussion process. By the end of the volume, your students should be working together to improve their discussions. When setting goals for the improvement of your Touchpebbles Discussions, always ask for your students' help identifying problems with the discussions and offering solutions.

MODIFYING THE TEACHER'S GUIDE

As a teacher, you know from daily experience that every group of students differs from every other group. Each discussion group progresses at its own pace and must deal with unique dynamics. You must tailor your approach to each group. Feel free to modify the suggestions in this *Teacher's Guide* to meet your group's needs. Although Touchstones strongly recommends that you move through the lessons in the order presented in this volume, the following are suggestions for modifying the lessons to meet the specific needs of your group:

- Have the students discuss their discussions.
- Ask the students to brainstorm ways to improve their discussions.
- Spend two sessions on a particular lesson before moving on.
- Take some time at the end of class for the students to write a journal entry about the discussion.
- Ask the students to create opening questions.

Seeking Additional Support. This *Teacher's Guide* is your primary support as a Touchpebbles Discussion leader, but it is only one of several possible resources.

The Touchstones Web site offers information about all Touchstones programs. Furthermore, the Touchstones staff is readily available to answer any questions that you may have, and they can be reached at the address and phone number below. Finally, remember to consult with other discussion leaders. Sharing your experiences is a great way to find out how others have handled difficult discussion situations.

> Touchstones Discussion Project
> 522 Chesapeake Avenue
> Annapolis, Maryland 21403
> 800-456-6542
> (fax) 410-974-8233
> www.touchstones.org
> info@touchstones.org

Lesson 1

A Different Kind of Class

PURPOSE

Today you will introduce your students to the format and ground rules of a Touchpebbles class.

Students will:
- Experience their first discussion class.
- Discuss the ground rules and their expectations of the Touchpebbles class.

INTRODUCTION

Your students and you are about to undertake a new activity—a Touchpebbles Discussion. In students' past classroom experience, you have been the most important person in the room. The students have depended on you for information, discipline, calling on speakers, and covering material. Even in cooperative activities, you have set the goals for their tasks. However, in Touchpebbles Discussions, your students will gradually learn to take over these functions. Because this is a very gradual process, you will be constantly shifting gears. Sometimes you will give students definite tasks and organize the activities as you do in regular class sessions; at other times, you will allow students a great deal of leeway to explore ideas, face problems, and struggle to learn from one another.

The best way to introduce students to Touchpebbles Discussions is to allow them to experience the process. In all cases, a mere list of ground rules is simply too abstract to be helpful. Even if your students understand rules like "do not interrupt when others are speaking," they will be unable to follow them at first. This situation occurs because following the rules requires developing new habits and skills. The students will acquire these new skills by first experiencing the difficulties and problems that arise when the rules are violated and then working out the solutions. This task is itself a valuable educational experience and you should not deprive them of it. You should keep this long-range goal of skill development in mind and not feel frustrated in the early stages when problems arise. In these first sessions, your task will be to help the students remain patient with themselves, focus them on the problems, and assist them in exploring solutions to the problems.

The Touchpebbles Ground Rules
1. We do not raise our hands when we want to speak.
2. We speak to everyone in the class and not just to our neighbors and friends.
3. We do not interrupt when others are speaking.
4. We listen carefully to what other students say.

The four rules should be written on a large sheet of paper or on a section of the board and kept displayed. Periodically, even during non–Touchpebbles activities, you might refer to these ground rules as a way of helping students keep them in mind. You might use those occasions to talk about the reasons behind the rules. In this first activity, you will be acting more like a guide than a discussion leader, although you should always permit discussion if the students take the initiative. Eventually they will follow the rules and create additional ones because they will have concretely experienced the problems that discussion brings to the surface. This will be an exercise in creating a learning community.

Lesson Summary

This lesson will not begin with your handing out a list of ground rules. Instead, exploring the need for ground rules will be part of the lesson's structure. Today's text contains a partial description of a Touchpebbles class. Some characteristics of this class are mentioned, whereas others are not and should be brought up by you. For example, the story describes how, in Cheryl's brother's class, the students sit in a circle. However, the story does not mention that they don't raise their hands. The fact that no one raises his or her hands in a Touchpebbles Discussion is something you should mention to the students at the start of today's class. At the beginning of the period, have the students sit in a circle and tell them that you are going to read them a story and that the entire group will talk about it. Tell them that when they want to talk, they should *not* raise their hands.

The story not only describes the class, it also brings up certain attitudes that the students have toward such a class. Since the Touchpebbles class is a different sort of class, students have definite reactions to it. Some students initially object to Touchpebbles simply because it is different; others respond positively precisely because it is different. Some of these attitudes are mentioned in the story. For example, in the story, two students who are good at giving correct answers are skeptical and scornful about such a class. This attitude arises because they get praise and approval under the conventional format in which answers are true or false or right or wrong. Such students are usually able to pick the answer the teacher has in mind. Conversely, a student who causes problems in regular classes is excited about the prospect of speaking when he or she wishes. Other attitudes not mentioned in the story could come up in the course of your class discussion.

Remember that today's meeting is your students' first attempt at a discussion. The students will behave as they always behave, and it will take time to create the environment for a fruitful discussion. However, even in this first phase, the students are learning to look at themselves from multiple perspectives. You should encourage the group to look at themselves as students in regular teacher-centered sessions and then compare that image with how they will be in a new form of class in which they are more responsible for the direction of the class.

Possible Questions to Raise

- Can you describe the kind of class that Cheryl talks about?
- What do you think that kind of class would be like?
- How is talking with your friends different from talking in class? How is it the same?
- Which ground rule do you think will be the most difficult to follow? Why?

Lesson 1: A Different Kind of Class

Lesson Plan 1

Activity   Time

1. **ARRANGE CLASSROOM** .... 5 min.
   - Ask your students to sit in a circle. You should sit in the circle too.
   - Briefly tell the class that you will read them a story and that they will talk about it with you and with one another. They are not to raise their hands.

2. **TEXT** .... 5 min.
   - Read the text aloud while students read along silently.
   - Mention other characteristics of the different kind of class.
   - Focus the discussion of the text on these characteristics, although you should give students a great deal of latitude to bring up differences between this new type of class and regular class sessions.

3. **INDIVIDUAL WORK** .... 8 min.
   - Read the worksheet aloud and explain the directions.
   - Ask the students to complete the worksheet.
   - During this phase, assist the students as you would in a regular class activity.

4. **SMALL GROUP WORK** .... 7 min.
   - Put the students in small groups according to the letters they write down for question 2 in the Individual Work. The activity asks the students to work together to solve the problem.
   - Since this is their first attempt at working together in groups, it is OK if they do not fully complete their task.

5. **DISCUSSION** .... 8 min.
   - Ask students to volunteer their responses to question 1 in the Individual Work.
   - After you have heard the different perspectives, it is especially important for you to have the group consider in turn how each problem could be solved. This will elicit their answers to the Small Group Work.

6. **INTRODUCE AND DISCUSS THE GROUND RULES** .... 7 min.
   - At the end of the class, spend a few minutes going over the ground rules.

Total: 40 minutes

A Different Kind of Class
(STUDENT VOLUME, PAGE 1)

About one minute after the bell rang, the students in Mrs. Green's second grade class realized that today was unusual. Mrs. Green was always in the room when they arrived. But today she was not there. The students were there alone. They began whispering to one another, hoping that someone knew what was going on. Mrs. White, the principal, came to the room and suddenly everyone was quiet. "Students," she said, "Mrs. Green will be late today, so I want you to read quietly until she comes." The students tried to read quietly, but before long the class was noisy again. Tommy, a student who always got himself in trouble, stood up and said, "If we don't quiet down, the principal will come back and I know I'll get blamed."

"What should we do?" asked Judy, the student who always knew the answers to Mrs. Green's questions. She was trying to put Tommy on the spot.

"I don't know. Why don't we try to hold class ourselves?" he said, annoyed.

"OK, I'll be the teacher," said Judy, jumping out of her seat. When the other students saw Judy jump up, they began to make noise again, showing her that they didn't want her to take over. "If you don't want me to lead, then someone else can do it," she said angrily. No one responded and the whispering began again.

As the noise increased, a student named Cheryl became nervous and spoke up. "I have an idea. My brother is in the sixth grade. Once a week in his class, everyone moves the chairs into a circle. The teacher reads a story and asks a question. Then the class starts talking about the story."

"What do they need to talk about it for?" asked Judy. "Doesn't anyone know the answer to the teacher's question?"

"My brother told me that the question isn't like the questions in regular classes," answered Cheryl. "It's not clear whether there's just one answer or whether the teacher even knows the answer. The teacher's question is mostly to get the group thinking and talking."

"Sounds pretty silly to me," said John, who, like Judy, always raised his hand with answers. "That would make the class just a lot of people who don't know the answer talking to one another. What's the point?"

"My brother said they talk about their own ideas, get to change their minds if they want to, and find out all kinds of things from one another," said Cheryl, looking directly at John and Judy. "People who seem dumb at first because they don't know the teacher's answers turn out to have really interesting things to say, and some kids who usually know all the answers find out that they can learn from other students."

"Sounds great," said Tommy. "You mean it's really not just figuring out the right answer?"

"That's right. The class learns to work together. Everybody has lots of ideas and they help one another. They never know exactly what they'll talk about. Sometimes they talk about what happened in the story, sometimes they talk about

Lesson 1: A Different Kind of Class

similar things that happened to them, and sometimes they talk about their own ideas."

"Why don't we do it?" said Steve, a student who usually never talked in class. "Mrs. Green read us a story yesterday about a judge. We could talk about that. And I have a question to start."

As Steve was about to ask his question, Mrs. Green came into the room. "Sorry I'm late," she said. "What have you been doing?"

John quickly raised his hand, and when Mrs. Green motioned to him, he said, "We've just been waiting."

"That's not true," said Tommy. "We were going to have a class on the story about the judge that you read to us yesterday. Steve was going to ask us a question and we were all going to talk about it." Others in the class made it clear that they all agreed. Mrs. Green looked pleased and said, "Well, Steve, why don't we talk about the story? What is your question?"

Worksheet 1: A Different Kind of Class

INDIVIDUAL WORK

1. In the story, Cheryl describes her brother's class. In that class, the sit in a circle and talk to one another without raising their hands. Below are some problems that often occur in such classes. Mark an "✘" next to the one that you think is the worst problem, and mark a "✔" next to the one that you think is the least serious problem.

   _____ a) Students sitting next to each other will talk to each other instead of the whole group.

   _____ b) Many students will talk at the same time.

   _____ c) Some students will talk all the time.

   _____ d) Some students will be afraid to talk.

   _____ e) Some students will talk only to their friends.

2. Which group would you be in? For example, if you think you might talk too much, you would be in group c. If you are willing to talk only to your friends, you would be in group e.

   I think I would be in group _____.

SMALL GROUP WORK

How could your group correct the problem that your group members identified? (You don't have to write down anything; just think about how you would solve the problem.)

Lesson 2

The Judge
A Tale from West Africa

PURPOSE

This week's lesson begins highlighting some of the common issues you and your students will address in the process of forming a discussion group. It achieves this objective by focusing on the subject of a judge.

Students will:
- Explore characteristics that a good judge might have.
- Discuss their own experiences with fair and unfair judgments.
- Practice making judgments in small groups, and discuss the experience.

INTRODUCTION

One of the hardest tasks for children and adults to undertake is to recognize their own particular interests, desires, and concerns and to control them. Each of us, every day, struggles with the differences between what we believe and what is true and between what we want to do and what is right to do. *Touchpebbles Volume A* focuses on these issues and helps students develop the skill of distinguishing between their own ideas and what is true and between their own desires and what is just and fair. This skill is developed through two routes. The first route enables the students to become aware that each of us possesses a unique perspective on the world. To deal with many of the texts, worksheets, and discussions in Touchpebbles, they will have to depart from their own point of view and adopt different ones. This process will involve exercising their imaginations. The second route will explore how to move from identifying the variety of perspectives to analyzing what may underlie, unite, or be implied by these perspectives. This process will involve students in evaluating evidence, making inferences, and using critical thinking. These skills are necessary for every aspect of their future lives, from understanding science and using technology to becoming involved citizens, choosing professions, and acting in cooperation with others.

Lesson 2: The Judge

Although only some of your students will be familiar with judges in courtrooms, either from their own experience or from TV, all of them will have had experience with the role judges play. From their early years, they have undoubtedly been involved in disputes and disagreements that needed the assistance of others to resolve. They therefore have had firsthand experience of how difficult it is to take on any distance from one's interests and perspectives to appreciate another's viewpoint. Usually in these situations, students have called upon a parent, another friend, or an adult to assist them in solving the problem or the dispute. Each disputant probably hoped that this "judge" would agree with his or her viewpoint. Of course, it is generally impossible for a judge to agree with both sides. Implicitly through such experiences, students have gradually come to recognize a judge as someone who is expected to represent what is right, fair, and true.

LESSON SUMMARY

This week's text and worksheet helps students confront these issues of fairness and truth. The story concerns two mice that must divide a piece of cheese. Because they disagree about how to do it—perhaps one piece of cheese looked more appealing than the other or each mouse wanted to cheat to obtain a bigger share—the mice seek the help of a third person, or judge. However, the story shows one of the crucial ways in which a judge can be unfair. Judges are expected to be both neutral between the parties in a disagreement and able to separate themselves from their own interests and perspectives. In the story, this latter criterion does not hold. The story shows that the judge may be no better than the mice. Judges are simply other people and they too may have the same difficulty as those whose dispute they are trying to resolve: they might want what the disputants want. In the story, the monkey also wants the cheese and finds a way to use his position as judge to get it. As a result, the mice must ask themselves why they were not able to settle the dispute without calling in a third person. If each mouse could have appreciated the perspective of the other, they would not have lost the cheese.

This dilemma brings up another aspect of asking someone to act as a judge. When there is a dispute, often each person has some merit to his or her position. It therefore happens that a judge who acts fairly will decide that each party is both right and wrong. Since neither party is likely to get everything that is desired, why bring in a judge who may act unfairly and cause both parties to lose everything? In this week's class, you should encourage students to bring up such instances from their experience. You might ask them to describe disputes and disagreements and explain how they dealt with them. The worksheet, which is to be completed before the text is read, will help the students focus on these issues by placing them in a similar situation. Each student is asked to draw a cat. In small groups, some of the students are selected to act as judges. The judges will decide which drawings are the best. After the judging, the students can consider how they chose the judges and what problems judges face.

Lesson 2: The Judge

POSSIBLE QUESTIONS TO RAISE
- Was it hard to select a judge?
- How did you pick a judge?
- Was it easy for the judge to decide?
- Do you think it is hard for judges to be fair? Why or why not?
- What kinds of qualities does a good judge have?
- Have you ever been in a situation in which someone was an unfair judge?
- Can you think of a time when you judged a situation unfairly?

Lesson 2: The Judge

LESSON PLAN 2

Activity   Time

1. **ARRANGE CLASSROOM** .... 5 min.
   - Ask your students to sit in a circle.
   - Pass out the worksheet.

2. **INDIVIDUAL WORK** .... 10 min.
   - Explain that the students' first task is to draw a picture of a cat. The drawing can be in pencil, pen, or crayon.
   - Question 2 asks them what characteristics they want in a judge. You may need to read each category to students to make sure they understand the options.

3. **SMALL GROUP WORK** .... 8 min.
   - Divide the class into small groups of four or five students.
   - Have each group select on group member to judge which drawing is best.
   - The judge should consider his or her picture with the rest.

4. **TEXT** .... 2 min.
   - Ask students to form the large circle again.
   - Read the text aloud as students read along silently.

5. **DISCUSSION**... 15 min.
   - Begin the discussion by asking the students when they last needed help to settle an argument. Focus them on what advice they would give the mice. After hearing some responses, have students describe their experiences working in small groups.

Total: 40 minutes

Worksheet 2: The Judge

 INDIVIDUAL WORK

1. In the space below or on the back of this sheet, draw the best picture that you can of a cat. (The cat can be sleeping, standing, sitting, eating, or doing anything else. You choose.)

2. What qualities should a judge have? Check TWO of the characteristics that you think are most important.

   The judge must be ...

   - ❏ biggest
   - ❏ kindest
   - ❏ your best friend
   - ❏ quietest
   - ❏ most thoughtful
   - ❏ most honest
   - ❏ bossiest
   - ❏ best at sports
   - ❏ funniest
   - ❏ strongest
   - ❏ oldest
   - ❏ smartest at schoolwork

 SMALL GROUP WORK

1. In your groups, choose one person to be the judge.
2. From among all the pictures, including the judge's, the judge should decide which picture is best.
3. Does everyone agree with the judge's decision?

Lesson 2: The Judge

The Judge
A Tale from West Africa
(STUDENT VOLUME, PAGE 5)

Two mice stole a large chunk of cheese. Both wanted to have what they thought was their fair share. But neither of them trusted the other to divide the cheese fairly. So they went to the lion, the king of all the animals. "King, we want to divide this cheese, but we can't do it fairly. We can't agree on what is fair. Please help us." The lion frowned at the mice because he was very busy but believed it was his duty to help. "I'll send you to the monkey. He's the judge and will help you, but it would be better if you could do it yourselves. Once you bring in a judge, many new problems might come up." But the mice wanted the monkey, and so the king sent them to his law court.

The monkey was seated in a big chair behind a large table. The mice asked for his help in dividing the cheese. The monkey said, "Of course I'll be the judge if you want me to." He sent his helper for a scale and a knife. With the knife, he cut the cheese so that one piece was much bigger than the other. Then he ate some of the bigger piece. The mice asked him what he was doing. "I'm eating from this piece so that it will be equal to the smaller piece," he said. He ate so much that when he put both pieces on the scale again, the one that used to be smaller was now bigger. So he began to eat from that piece. The mice now realized that the monkey planned to eat all the cheese. They said, "Give us what's left, O Judge, and we will divide it fairly." But the monkey said, "No. You will fight each other and then King Lion will be angry with me." So the monkey went on eating until all the cheese was gone. Then one mouse turned to the other and said, "Why didn't we trust each other and cut the cheese ourselves?"

Lesson 3

The Camel and the Jackal
A Tale from India

PURPOSE
Cooperation and conflict are central aspects of any group discussion. To form a good discussion group, participants must learn how to cooperate with one another and to address instances of conflict. This work begins with today's lesson.
Students will:
- Examine a story in which two characters refuse to cooperate.
- Discuss how the characters might have resolved their conflict.
- Relate the text to their own experiences with conflict and cooperation.

INTRODUCTION
The opposite of disagreement and conflict is cooperation. If the mice in Lesson 2 had been able to cooperate, they would not have needed a judge and would not have lost the cheese. However, cooperation is very difficult to achieve, especially if you don't know or don't like the person with whom you are to cooperate. All too often, someone in the group will try to control or dominate —they will stand out by being funny or bossy or by finding other ways to resist working with others. Genuine cooperation requires a great deal of self-understanding and understanding of others and a variety of skills and attitudes that will be practiced throughout Touchpebbles classes. Some of these skills, for example, not interrupting when another student speaks, will be worked on gradually during this year's work. Fundamental attitudes, such as learning that one can only achieve one's own goals when others achieve theirs, will take years to understand and master.

> **BENCHMARK**
> One of the first signs of group formation is that your students are talking to one another rather than through you.

In the past two lessons, you and your students have probably experienced both disagreement and cooperation. In the case of disagreement, your students

Lesson 3: The Camel and the Jackal

might have looked to you to judge or mediate. When they cooperated, however, your students no longer needed you to resolve their disagreements; rather, they needed you to assist them in setting goals and help them realize how much they have accomplished. To a great extent, the themes of the texts and the worksheets mirror the procedures of the discussion class. The texts give the students a tangible way to talk about such abstract issues as cooperation and conflict. Encourage the students to use the texts and worksheets to analyze their behavior.

Lesson Summary

In the story, the camel and the jackal are both hungry and need one another to get food. To cross the river to get the food he wants, the jackal requires the help of the camel. To find the sugarcane he wants, the camel requires the help of the jackal. Once they reach the other side of the river and find the food, however their cooperation breaks down. The jackal no longer thinks of the camel's needs or his point of view. Instead, the jackal either intentionally or unintentionally makes enough noise to bring out the villagers who then beat the camel. When the jackal and camel leave, the camel refuses to cooperate and instead gets revenge by causing the jackal to drown.

Cooperation typically breaks down in discussion classes and in many daily activities, and it becomes necessary to decide whether any future cooperation is still possible. In the story, the jackal and camel would probably agree on the facts of the situation—the camel was beaten because the jackal howled and yelped. However, the two animals would probably disagree over why the jackal made the noise. The jackal claims he did it because of habit; he didn't decide to cause the camel pain. The camel either doesn't believe the jackal's explanation, or he believes it doesn't matter. Because the camel was hurt, he will take revenge. In completing the worksheet, the students consider this situation. They must decide how they would respond to being hurt and whether any circumstances exist in which future cooperation with those who hurt them would be possible.

Possible Questions to Raise

- Was it OK for the camel to drown the jackal?
- Was it OK for the jackal to make noise?
- Can you explain the jackal's behavior in a way so that the camel would be willing to help him in spite of the camel's being beaten?
- If someone hurts you by accident or without thinking, can you still cooperate with him or her? Why?
- Could the camel and jackal cooperate again if the jackal did what he did by accident?
- Can you think of a situation in which you made up with someone who hurt you? How did you do it?
- What would you have done if you were the camel in this story?
- What if the jackal made noise on purpose?
- After enemies are done fighting, can they ever work together again? How?

Lesson 3: The Camel and the Jackal

LESSON PLAN 3

Activity	Time
1. ARRANGE CLASSROOM	5 min.

- Ask your students to sit in a circle.
- Pass out the worksheet.

2. INDIVIDUAL WORK . . . . 8 min.

- Have the students complete questions 1 and 2.

3. TEXT . . . . 2 min.

- Read the story aloud as students read along silently.

4. DISCUSSION . . . . 13 min.

- Ask the students whether it was right for the camel to do what he did.
- Bring up other similar instances or encourage the students to recount situations in which they or someone they know well got even with another person and recount what happened.
- At the end of the discussion, ask the students to answer question 3 in the Individual Work.

5. SMALL GROUP WORK . . . . 7 min.

- After the students have completed the worksheet, divide the class into groups of four or five students. Each group should consist of students who gave the same answer to question 3 in the Individual Work.
- Have the small groups decide how the jackal could convince the camel not to drown him.

6. GROUP REPORTS . . . . 5 min.

- Bring the students back into the large group and have each group report on what they decided.

Total: 40 minutes

TOUCHPEBBLES VOLUME A

Worksheet 3: The Camel and the Jackal

INDIVIDUAL WORK

1. One person hurts another. The person who is hurt doesn't know if it was done on purpose, without thinking, or just by accident. What should the person who was hurt do about it? Mark the best thing to do with "✔." Mark the reaction you think is the worst with "✘."

    The person who was hurt should—

    _____ a) get angry, but do nothing.

    _____ b) get angry and get back at the other person later.

    _____ c) get angry and hit the other person.

    _____ d) tell the other person that he or she is angry and not to do it again.

    _____ e) ask the other person why he or she did it.

    _____ f) some other reaction (write it here):_____

2. Which is worse: when someone hurts another person on purpose or by accident?

    ❑ on purpose   ❑ by accident

Stop here. Answer question 3 *after* your teacher reads the story to you.

3. Did the jackal run around, yelp, and howl on purpose or by accident?

    ❑ on purpose   ❑ by accident

SMALL GROUP WORK

How could the jackal convince the camel not to drown him? Discuss this question with your group, and have one member of the group write the group's answer below.

The Camel and the Jackal
A Tale from India
(STUDENT VOLUME, PAGE 7)

A camel and a jackal, an animal who is like a small wild dog, met one day and talked about what they liked to eat. The camel said he liked sugarcane, and the Jackal said he liked fish and crabs that he got from the river's edge. The jackal said, "I can't swim. But if you carry me over that river, I'll show you where there is sugarcane, and I'll have fresh fish and crabs."

The camel agreed, so he swam across the river carrying the jackal on his back. The jackal showed the camel where the sugarcane was growing, and they both began their meals. But because the jackal was much smaller than the camel, he finished his meal of fish and crabs before the camel had eaten three or four mouthfuls of sugarcane. The camel was still very hungry.

As soon as the jackal had finished, he began running all over the sugarcane field, howling and yelping as loudly as he could. The local villagers awoke and thought animals were in their fields stealing crops. They hurried out and found the camel eating their sugarcane, but the jackal had hidden. They caught the camel and beat him half to death.

When the villagers had left, the jackal came out of hiding and said to the camel, "Let's go home."

The camel said, "Jump on my back and I'll swim back across the river." When they were in the middle of the river, the camel said, "That was selfish and mean of you to howl and yelp after you finished your dinner. I had barely started my dinner when the villagers came and beat me with sticks and whips. Why did you make such a noise?"

"I don't know," said the jackal. "It's just something I always do. It's a habit. I always sing and run after a good meal."

The camel said, "How strange! I have a strong need to roll over in the water whenever I'm swimming."

"Oh, no!" cried the jackal. "Why?"

"I don't know," replied the camel. "It's just something I always do. You know, it's a habit." So he rolled over in the water. The jackal fell off and drowned, but the camel swam to the opposite shore.

Lesson 4

The Clever Thief
A Tale from Korea

PURPOSE

All fundamental changes are difficult and require comparing our opinions about ourselves with what others say honestly about us. This comparison is especially hard when what is said is critical of our thoughts, manner, or ideas. In Lesson 3, the students had to put themselves in someone else's place. In this lesson, they will practice listening to and exploring what others think of them.

Students will:
- Practice evaluating their, and a partner's, behavior in Touchpebbles classes.
- Consider a story in which another person's words and actions motivate people to examine their own character.
- Discuss the difficulties and benefits of examining one's character with the help of other people.

INTRODUCTION

In regular content classes, a premium is often placed on students' ability to get correct answers. Teachers try to communicate facts and ideas to students and gauge success by students' answers in classes and on tests. Touchpebbles Discussions are quite different. Your priority is not to cover material but rather, your main task in these classes is to develop students' skills and foster new intellectual and behavioral habits. As a result, your students—in addition to increasing their pool of information—will change on deeper levels. These changes will make all your students able to gain more in regular content classes. The students will learn to share responsibility with you for their education. But achieving this goal requires a fundamental change in their attitudes about themselves.

Lesson 4: The Clever Thief

All your students are familiar with certain ways in which they have changed over the past few years. Being embarrassed, fearing being mocked, being accused of acting like a baby—all these are powerful motivators for changing behavior. In many cases, changes in students' behavior or attitudes occurred because they came to see themselves as others whom they respected, loved, or feared saw them. Deciding to change involves adopting a point of view that is not only different from one's own but also critical of one's behavior. This ability to accept criticism is fundamental to all true learning. The typical expression of this recognition is to feel shame. When we feel ashamed of ourselves, we are acknowledging two views of ourselves. One view is how we presently are and behave; the other is how we wish we could be, and, at least at the moment of feeling shame, how we aspire to become. The class will begin to consider issues of criticism, shame, and change with this week's text and worksheet.

Lesson Summary

The story tells about a thief who finally gets caught. While he is in prison, he begins to regret his life and wishes to change. He devises a plan to free himself, return home, and live a different life. His plan involves confronting the rulers of his country and showing them that, if they could see themselves from a new perspective, they would see that they are no different from him. He presents the king with what he claims is a magical plum pit. He says it will produce golden plums if it is planted by someone who has never cheated or stolen. The king and his ministers do not accept it. All of them remember times when they, like the thief, stole or cheated. The king feels shame and frees the thief in gratitude for the lesson he has learned. That feeling of shame was, according to the king, a precious gift. In the class discussion, have the students focus on whether they believe this shame was indeed a precious gift.

The worksheet presents the students with a list of typical ways people behave in discussions. Some students talk too much whereas others are too shy to speak. Students are asked to choose the phrases that most accurately describe their behavior. Some of the judgments students are asked to make about themselves are quite strong and critical, for example, "I talk too much" or "I interrupt people." But the students should be able to make these self-judgments. Then the students are paired. Each student completes the Pair Work. The judgments in the Pair Work are purposely much less harsh or critical than those in the Individual Work because they are judgments about the students' partners. The students, still in pairs, then compare and discuss the judgments and try to agree on which best describes each of them. This activity forces them to consider and respond to a different perspective. You might begin the discussion by asking whether the students think the king will change and why. In the course of the discussion, refer back to the worksheets and the paired activity. You can ask the students whether they discovered anything new about themselves and how they will go about changing.

Lesson 4: The Clever Thief

POSSIBLE QUESTIONS TO RAISE

- How do you think the king will be different from now on?
- Do you think the king would have realized his faults if the thief had not said what he did?
- Was the king right to set the thief free? Why?
- What was the hardest part of the paired activity?
- Why did the king tell the thief that he had given him a wonderful gift?
- Was it hard to decide what you want to improve on? Why?
- Do you think the plum pit is really magical, as the thief says?

Lesson 4: The Clever Thief

Lesson Plan 4

| Activity | Time |

1. **Arrange Classroom**..5 min.
   - Have the students sit in a circle.
   - Pass out the worksheet.

2. **Individual Work**..5 min.
   - Ask the students to complete the Individual Work. You may wish to start this session by asking the students whether these behaviors have occurred in the first three Touchpebbles classes.

3. **Pair Work**..7 min.
   - Divide the class into pairs and have the students answer the statements about their partner.
   - In pairs, have the students consider and compare their responses about themselves with the judgments of their partner. They should try to agree on one item for each partner.

4. **Small Group Work**..10 min.
   - Divide the class into groups of five or six students.
   - Have the group consider how each group member can be a better member of the large group discussion.

5. **Text**...2 min.
   - Read the text aloud as students read along silently.

6. **Discussion**..11 min.
   - Open the discussion by asking whether the students think the king will change. Why or how?

Total: 40 minutes

Worksheet 4: The Clever Thief

INDIVIDUAL WORK

Check the items that best describe how you are in your Touchpebbles Discussions.

- ❑ I talk too much.
- ❑ I don't talk enough.
- ❑ I interrupt people.
- ❑ I only listen to people I like.
- ❑ If people don't like what I say, I am unhappy.
- ❑ I talk to my neighbors.
- ❑ I try to help other people talk.
- ❑ I admit when I'm wrong.

PAIR WORK

Check the items that best describe how you see your partner in Touchpebbles Discussions.

- ❑ My partner should speak more.
- ❑ My partner needs to listen more carefully.
- ❑ My partner should help others speak.
- ❑ My partner needs to let others finish talking.
- ❑ My partner should let other people speak more.
- ❑ My partner should try harder to listen to everyone who speaks.
- ❑ My partner shouldn't be unhappy if others don't like what he or she says.
- ❑ My partner needs to admit when he or she is wrong.

SMALL GROUP WORK

Together, decide what each of you needs to improve on the most. The answer might be different for each person in your group, but the entire group should help each group member decide what he or she needs to improve.

I want to improve on: _____.

The Clever Thief
A Tale from Korea
(STUDENT VOLUME, PAGE 9)

Many years ago, there was a thief who had never been caught by the police. He grew rich but, because he thought he was so clever, he became careless. One day he was caught stealing some spices from a shop. He was arrested and sent to jail. He kept trying to escape, but the prison was so strong that he finally gave up. For a year he sat in his cell. At first, he just regretted his carelessness but then began to feel that he had wasted his life and wished he could begin again. He thought about all the rich and powerful people in his country and how he could have been one of them if he had not chosen to be a thief. As he thought about what the king and the other powerful people in his country were really like, he made up a plan to get out of jail. However, he promised himself that if he succeeded, he would live a quiet, honest life.

The next day he told the jailer that he needed to see the king. He said he had a great gift for the king. Startled by the request, the jailer took the prisoner to the royal palace. The king was on his throne surrounded by his helpers and his generals. When the king asked him what he wanted, the old thief said he had a great gift for him. "If you waste my time," said the king, "I will have you killed." "I have a wonderful gift for you," said the thief, and he presented a beautifully wrapped box to his ruler. The king opened the box and found a plum pit. "How dare you waste my time and bring me something so ordinary," said the king.

"My king, this is a very special pit. The person who plants it will reap golden plums," said the thief. The king became interested but asked, "Why don't you plant it?" "That's the sad part of it," said the old thief. "Many years ago I stole it, but it only works if planted by someone who has never stolen or cheated. That is why I have brought it to you." The king shook his head sadly and remained silent. He was an honest man but remembered how he had once stolen a few pennies from his mother when he was a child. "What about some of your helpers or generals?" asked the thief, looking at the important people surrounding the king.

None of them answered because they all remembered that they had used their power to steal and cheat others at some time in their lives. The room remained silent until finally the old thief said, "You all cheat and steal and yet I am sent to jail for stealing a few spices in the market. In fact, I am better than you are because at least I know I am a thief and have become ashamed of myself." The king lowered his head for a moment in shame. Then he

Lesson 4: The Clever Thief

said, "Sir, you are free. You have in fact given me a wonderful present. Sometimes kings and powerful people forget that we are just like everyone else. We will remember the lesson you taught us." The thief was pleased at this result but wondered whether these rulers would learn this lesson. Still, he returned to his home to fulfill his promise to himself to live a quiet and honest life.

DISCUSSION EVALUATION SHEET 1

An important part of leading Touchstones Discussions is effectively strategizing and choosing goals for each class. Maybe one or two students are dominating the large group discussion, or perhaps you have seen many of the skills in practice, and you want to start working on new skills. We are placing these evaluation sheets periodically throughout this volume to provide you with opportunities to recognize the progress your group is making and the obstacles you are encountering. These evaluations may be very helpful part of your planning and strategizing, since they will give you an opportunity to assess the needs of the group and choose goals for the upcoming sessions.

Each of the questions below relates to goals that the group should have been working toward in recent sessions. If you think that any of these goals are not being met, you should choose to work on those goals in the coming discussions. Remember that these goals are never met in any one session. Working toward the goals is a continual process, and at this early stage, it is likely that work will still need to be done on all these goals.

In addition, these questions always look both backward and forward. That is, they ask about goals that should already have been worked on and goals that lie ahead of the group. Since no two groups will follow the same path through these goals, this format should help you strategize most effectively. Use the space below to clarify or expand your answer. Maybe some students are and some students are not meeting the goal, or maybe the goals are usually met, but in one or two discussions they have not been. Refer to your answers as you prepare the upcoming discussions.

Are at least 60 percent of the students participating in each discussion?
❑ Never ❑ Sometimes ❑ Often ❑ Always

Have all the students participated in at least one discussion?
❑ Yes ❑ No

Are all the students participating in the small groups?
❑ Never ❑ Sometimes ❑ Often ❑ Always

Are the students relating their experience to the topic at hand?
❑ Never ❑ Sometimes ❑ Often ❑ Always

Lesson 5

Hound and Hunter
by Winslow Homer

PURPOSE

In Lesson 5, the students will discuss the differences between visual and intellectual perspective.

Students will:
- View a painting, and discuss the relationships among the images.
- Create a story about the painting.
- Compare their stories, and discuss the differences that arise.

INTRODUCTION

Touchpebbles Volume A is concerned with developing in students the ability to understand and articulate different perspectives. In its most common meaning, perspective refers to the way we see an object—it depends on our position. People looking at the same object from different positions see it differently. By studying these differences, painters are able to paint good approximations of the way we actually see things in the world.

Over time, the term perspective has grown to include the entire range of differences in intellectual attitudes and beliefs that people have about particular subjects or issues—or about the world itself. Just as visual perspective depends on the physical position of the viewer's eye, intellectual perspective depends on the cultural, economic, social, and educational position of the individual.

LESSON SUMMARY

The text is a painting by Winslow Homer. Have the students look at the painting before they complete the worksheet. They will be able to identify many objects represented, for example, the dog, the young boy, the deer, the boat, and the shoreline. Have the students concentrate on the spatial relationships among the objects,

Lesson 5: Hound and Hunter

for instance, how far the canoe is from the dog and from the different parts of the shore. Encourage the students to comment on any other relationships they notice, for example, the size of the canoe or the dog. This exercise will give them some practice in "reading" how objects are represented in pictorial space. You might also have them compare the geometric center of the painting (approximately three-quarters of an inch to the left of and slightly above the boy's eyes) with the visual center, which is a triangle, the three vertices of which are the heads of the boy, the deer, and the dog.

In the worksheet, the students are asked to make some decisions about the painting, for example, the season of the year and the expression on the boy's face. This activity gives the students some practice in interpreting the content of the painting and sets the stage for the principal activity of the class. In small groups, the students will create a short story about the painting. These stories will undoubtedly differ from one group to the next. Try to allow enough time for the small groups to report their stories and supporting evidence to the large group and also enough time for the class to comment on the differences. So that you have enough time to focus on each group's story, you may want to extend this class over two sessions.

POSSIBLE QUESTIONS TO RAISE

- Which is easier to agree on: what the painting is of or which story is correct? Why?
- Do your stories about the painting tell you as much as the painting does?
- Can you come up with any way to decide which story is best? If so, how?
- What is the boy doing?
- How did the deer get into the water?
- Is the deer dead or alive?
- What is the dog doing?

Lesson 5: Hound and Hunter

Lesson Plan 5

| Activity | Time |

1. **Arrange Classroom** .... 5 min.
2. **Painting** .... 1 min.
   - Have the students form a large circle.
3. **Discussion** .... 8 min.
   - Have the students identify as many things as they can, such as the dog, the boy, the deer, the log on the shore, and so forth.
   - Ask how far apart things seem to be from one another: How far away is the dog from the boy? How far is it to the shore? Is the dog closer to the boy than to the shore?
   - Ask the students where in the painting they tend to focus their attention.
   - At this point, you might show the students the geometric center of the painting (found at the intersection of the diagonals drawn from the corners) and have them compare that center with the triangle of action formed by the heads of the boy, the dog, and the deer.
4. **Individual Work** .... 5 min.
   - Pass out the worksheets and give the students a minute more to look at the painting.
   - Ask them to answer the questions in the Individual Work. Tell the students that they are going to write a story about the painting.
5. **Small Group** .... 11 min.
   - Divide the class into groups of three or four students.
   - Tell them to compare their answers from the Individual Work and agree on an answer for each question.
   - Have each group pick one person or a volunteer to write down the story that the group makes up together. Tell the group that they must have evidence from the painting to support their story.
6. **Group Reports** .... 10 min.
   - Bring the students back to the large circle.
   - Ask for volunteers to read their stories and point out what evidence they found in the painting to support their story.
   - Allow students to comment on the differences.
   - If a discussion of the painting begins, allow it to go on. If time allows, have all the groups read their stories.

Total: 40 minutes

TOUCHPEBBLES VOLUME A

Lesson 5: Hound and Hunter

Hound and Hunter
by Winslow Homer
(STUDENT VOLUME, PAGE 75)

The painting for this lesson is located on page 233.

Worksheet 5: Hound and Hunter

INDIVIDUAL WORK

Look at the painting for a few moments, then answer the questions below. Check the boxes that you think describe the painting. If what you think is not listed, you can write your own answers on the lines below.

a) Is the river flowing
- ❏ left to right,
- ❏ right to left?

b) Is the deer
- ❏ dead,
- ❏ wounded,
- ❏ struggling,
- ❏ swimming?

c) Is the boy
- ❏ angry,
- ❏ sad,
- ❏ excited,
- ❏ pleased?

d) Is the dog
- ❏ helping the boy,
- ❏ helping the deer,
- ❏ watching the boy?

e) Is the boy
- ❏ helping the deer,
- ❏ calling the dog,
- ❏ catching the deer for dinner?

f) Is the weather
- ❏ cold,
- ❏ warm,
- ❏ going to rain,
- ❏ going to be sunny?

Other thoughts:

_____
_____
_____
_____

TOUCHPEBBLES VOLUME A

SMALL GROUP WORK

1. In your group, compare your answers to the Individual Work and try to agree on them.
2. Together, create a story about the painting. Be sure to give the boy and the dog a name in your story.
3. Pick one person in your group to write down the story.
4. Pick one person in your group to read the story to the rest of the class. You will also need to point out the parts of the painting that you used to create your story.

Lesson 6

The Lion and the Mouse
by Aesop

PURPOSE

Lesson 6 asks students to consider the idea that different people possess different, but equally valuable, kinds of skills. One of the overarching goals of Touchpebbles is to help your students recognize the variety of skills their classmates possess and that all these different sets of skills are useful in a discussion.

Students will:
- Examine the relationship between liking an activity and being skilled in it.
- Discuss skills that they each would like to develop, and share strategies and ideas for developing them.
- Explore a text in which two unlikely partners help each other by using their very different skill sets.

INTRODUCTION

All your students differ from one another. Certain students read, write, speak, calculate, remember, or listen better than do others. Students are very aware of these differences. Often they say that they are good at—and therefore they like—certain activities. Or they say that they are bad at—and thus don't like—certain other activities. These two claims frequently go together, although one need not always precede the other. The students who read well generally enjoy reading; people who enjoy working with numbers often become good at mathematics. People often like what they're good at and are good at what they like. Unfortunately, the opposite—that people

> **BENCHMARK**
> Participation among your students is increasing in large group discussions so that on a given day, more than half of the students are contributing. Most, if not all, students are participating in small group work.

Lesson 6: The Lion and the Mouse

don't like what they are bad at and are bad at what they don't like—is also frequently true. If students believe this axiom, it can prevent them from learning because they will avoid activities that they don't like or in which they lack skills. Touchpebbles circumvents this impasse by helping students bridge the gap between skills they already possess and skills they lack. Touchpebbles also helps students see the importance and interdependence of many different kinds of skills.

In Touchpebbles Discussions, no one starts out more or less skilled than anyone else. This is because none of your students have had any systematic and sustained experience in genuine discussion. In addition, every student brings strengths and weaknesses to the group. For example, highly articulate children often have difficulty listening to others. Students who are behind in reading skills are often very sensitive listeners. The overall success of the class will depend on students' recognition that the skills they have as well as those they lack are necessary in a discussion. This recognition may be a difficult step for students to take. Good readers who listen poorly often imagine that others do not make statements that are worth listening to. Poor readers who listen well might think that no one cares what they think. Students will have to broaden their perspectives and realize that they need one another. The text and worksheet for this lesson will help your students begin to explore the ways in which they can learn from one another and the ways to develop the skills they lack.

Lesson Summary

Aesop's fable, "The Lion and the Mouse," is a classic example of two characters finding out that they can work with each other. The lion, the king of the jungle, is acknowledged by all the other animals to be the most powerful and skilled of them all. The lion here bears a similarity to those students who have clearly developed and well-recognized talents and skills. The mouse, who appears to have no important skills, might be compared to those students whose latent talents and abilities are not often recognized by anyone, possibly even themselves (although in the story the mouse is confident that he can help the lion at some later date). It is significant that the lion changes his opinion only when he is forced by a life-threatening situation to recognize the mouse's skills.

The worksheet asks the students to assess a list of skills on the basis of whether they are good at them or not. Then they must pick one thing they are not good at but would like to learn. In small groups, the students will discuss how they will become good at this skill. In many situations, students will receive ideas about how to improve from another person who possesses the skill that they would like to have. Frequently, this person will be someone they don't know very well. Thus, students can begin to recognize and respect the variety of skills distributed among their classmates. Significant change begins when someone can imagine being different.

Lesson 6: The Lion and the Mouse

POSSIBLE QUESTIONS TO RAISE

- What talents are important in a discussion class?
- Why does the lion laugh when the mouse says he would help him someday?
- Which is more important, listening or speaking? Why?
- What do you think the lion learned from this situation?
- What do you think the mouse learned?
- Have you ever experienced a situation similar to the one in the story?

Lesson 6: The Lion and the Mouse

Lesson Plan 6

| Activity | Time |

1. **Arrange Classroom** .... 5 min.
2. **Individual Work** .... 8 min.
   - Pass out the worksheets.
   - Have the students complete the section.
3. **Small Group Work** .... 15 min.
   - Divide the class into groups of three to five students.
   - Have group members discuss briefly with one another the skills they do and do not have.
   - After the students compare their impressions, ask them to move on to question 2. Each student should say what skills he or she would like to gain. The group will help each member figure out how he or she might get that skill.
4. **Text** .... 2 min.
   - Have the students return to the large circle.
   - Read the story aloud while the students read along silently. Give them another minute to read it again.
5. **Discussion** .... 10 min.
   - Ask the students how the two animals could help each other in the future.
   - After they have considered the story, turn their attention to their Touchpebbles Discussions. Ask them what skills are necessary to participate in discussions.

Total: 40 minutes

Worksheet 6: The Lion and the Mouse

INDIVIDUAL WORK

All of us have some things we are good at and some things we can't do or find difficult. Listed below are many different kinds of skills. For each skill, put a mark in the column that describes you. You must put at least one mark in the "Good at It" column and one mark in the "Not Good at It" column.

	Good at It	Not good at It	Don't care
a) Doing arithmetic	❏	❏	❏
b) Speaking clearly	❏	❏	❏
c) Running fast	❏	❏	❏
d) Helping others with chores	❏	❏	❏
e) Writing neatly	❏	❏	❏
f) Writing stories	❏	❏	❏
g) Keeping secrets	❏	❏	❏
h) Telling stories	❏	❏	❏
i) Playing a team sport	❏	❏	❏
j) Keeping my room clean	❏	❏	❏
k) Getting along with people	❏	❏	❏
l) Listening and remembering	❏	❏	❏
m) Making people laugh	❏	❏	❏

(S) SMALL GROUP WORK

1. Look back over the whole list of skills and pick the one skill that you are not good at now that you would like the most to become good at. Share your choice with your group.
2. Discuss in your group how you could become better at the skill you picked. If members of your group happen to be good at what you'd like to learn to do well, you might ask them how they learned to do it.

The Lion and the Mouse
by Aesop
(STUDENT VOLUME, PAGE 15)

Once a lion was lying asleep in the long grass near a river. A mouse who was hurrying home didn't notice him. The mouse brushed against the lion's whiskers and ran across his paw. The lion was a light sleeper. He was always ready to attack, even while sleeping. At the stirring of his whiskers, he awakened and caught the mouse with his other paw. He was about to make an end of the tiny creature who had disturbed him. However, he heard the mouse speak to him respectfully. "O King, forgive me. I didn't mean to interrupt your rest. I was hurrying so I didn't notice where I was going," said the mouse.

"And why should I care? You were careless and there are no second chances in the jungle," answered the lion.

"O King," answered the mouse, "if you let me go, I shall be grateful forever. Perhaps one day I will be able to help you."

The lion was so surprised at the mouse's reply that he roared with laughter. "You help me? A tiny mouse help the King of the Jungle? Impossible! But what you say is so funny that I'll let you go," and the lion lifted his paw and allowed the mouse to continue home.

A few weeks later, the mouse was again returning home when he heard a noise in the bushes. He was surprised to hear the lion roaring in pain. He inched closer to the sound and soon saw the reason. The lion was caught in a net set by hunters. The ropes surrounded him and each time he moved, they were drawn tighter. "Lion, O King, don't move. You're only making it worse. I'll be right there." The lion heard the mouse and looked ashamed at how careless he had been. "Now is your chance to laugh at me," said the King of the Beasts.

The mouse replied, "Lion, you once saved my life. I am forever grateful to you." At that, the mouse began to chew away at the ropes and before long was able to cut through the net. The lion was amazed to see how clever the little creature was. When the hole was large enough to escape, the lion jumped forward and then paused in front of the mouse. "Thank you, Mouse. You really were able to help me," he said as he looked at his tiny helper and then leapt into the forest.

Lesson 7

A Test of Strength
A Tale of the Fan Tribe of Africa

PURPOSE

One of the goals of Touchstones programs is to help students become aware of the way they form opinions and judgments about ideas and other people. This lesson's text provides an occasion for investigating this topic through a subject that all your students think about a lot—friendship.

Students will:
- Examine how they are different from and similar to those with whom they are already friends.
- Investigate whether friends must be equal to one another and, if so, in what ways.
- Discuss what it means to say that people are equal to one another.

INTRODUCTION

In the previous lesson, your students explored how they were different, how they each had different strengths and weaknesses, and how they might rely on other people's skills to compensate for their own limitations. An important question emerges out of these considerations: are we equal in spite of our differences? The claim that we are equal is the fundamental tenet of American society as manifested in the Declaration of Independence and the Constitution. However, this claim is very difficult to reconcile with the realities of our daily lives. It is almost impossible not to notice how we are different and thus to rank certain individual characteristics as more or less valuable and important. One of the results of believing that we are equal is that we treat one another with genuine respect; a consequence of believing that we are not equal is that we disrespect one another.

In your Touchpebbles meetings, you have probably been concerned with establishing a tone of respect among your students. In the early stages of any

Lesson 7: A Test of Strength

discussion group, many students pay attention primarily to what their friends say. They may often ignore the contributions of students whom they don't know or don't like. This situation is not surprising because friends usually respect one another and believe that they are basically equal. It's hard to imagine real friendship occurring between people who do not respect one another and who do not believe that they are equal in spite of their differences. However, in Touchpebbles Discussions, your students have started to learn new, surprising things about one another. Often students will find that someone who they either don't know or don't like will say something that is helpful or interesting. Gradually, a feeling of respect emerges. Achieving this respect requires the students to rethink various judgments that they have made about other students in the class.

Lesson Summary

The worksheet presents a list of characteristics, such as height and interest in music, and asks how important it is to the students that their friends share these characteristics. For many students, this exercise will be the first time they have ever thought about the underlying criteria they use when choosing friends. They could be surprised at what they consider important and unimportant about their friends. Some students will probably think some characteristics that are not on the list are more significant than ones that are, for example, whether or not someone is a kind, a good, or an honest person or fun to hang out with. In the discussion, you should give them the opportunity to bring up these characteristics.

The story explores issues of equality from a different angle. In the story, a turtle claims to be friends with a hippo and an elephant. They both laugh at him because they are so different from him. The turtle then challenges each one of them to a tug-of-war. By tricking the hippo and elephant, the turtle convinces them that he is equal to them in strength and becomes their friend. The story ends with the question of whether the turtle is indeed their equal. The turtle is clearly not equal to them in strength. But does the turtle's cleverness make up for his lack of strength so that, even though the three animals are different, they are nonetheless equal?

Possible Questions to Raise

- Are the turtle, the hippo and the elephant all equal to one another? Why or why not?
- What does it mean to say that two people are equal?
- Do we have to be similar to be equal?
- Are your friends very similar to you? In what ways are your friends equal to you?
- Why do you think the elephant and the hippo laughed at the idea of being friends with the turtle?
- Can you think of any friends that you have who are very different from you?
- Can you think of a way that the turtle might be telling the truth when he says that he is equal in power and strength to the hippo and the elephant?

Lesson 7: A Test of Strength

Lesson Plan 7

Activity   **Time**

1. ARRANGE CLASSROOM .... 5 min.
2. INDIVIDUAL WORK .... 5 min.
   - Pass out the worksheet.
   - Ask the students to answer question 1 on their own.
3. SMALL GROUP WORK .... 8 min.
   - Divide the class into groups of three to five students and ask group members to complete the Small Group Work and share their responses with one another.
4. GROUP REPORT... 5 min.
   - Bring students back to the large group.
   - Ask them to report on their work in the small groups.
5. TEXT .... 2 min.
   - Read the story aloud while students read along silently. .
6. DISCUSSION .... 15 min.
   - Begin by asking the group how important it is to them that they see their friends as equals.
   - After some discussion, ask the students to answer the question asked at the end of the story.

Total: 40 minutes

TOUCHPEBBLES VOLUME A

Worksheet 7: A Test of Strength

INDIVIDUAL WORK

Decide how important it is to you that your best friend is equal to you in each of the following ways. Next to each item, circle 1 if it is very important, 2 if it is kind of important, and 3 if it is not important at all.

	Very	Kind of	Not
Height (how tall you both are)	1	2	3
Weight (how heavy you both are)	1	2	3
Intelligence (how smart you both are)	1	2	3
Strength (how strong you both are)	1	2	3
Gender (both boys or both girls)	1	2	3
Background (families and houses similar)	1	2	3
Music (enjoy the same music)	1	2	3
Activities (enjoy doing the same things)	1	2	3
Language (you speak the same language)	1	2	3
Age (you are both the same age)	1	2	3

SMALL GROUP WORK

As a group, choose from the list above the most important way you should be equal with your best friend. Try to agree on just one way.

A Test of Strength
A Tale of the Fan Tribe of Africa
(STUDENT VOLUME, PAGE 17)

The turtle thought he was very wonderful. Wherever he went, he always would say, "We three—the elephant, the hippo, and I—are the greatest animals in the jungle. We three are equal in power and strength." When the elephant and hippo heard this claim, they both laughed. The story of their laughter got back to the turtle and angered him. "So, they laugh at me! I'll show them my power. Before long they'll realize that I'm equal to them. Soon they'll think of me as a friend."

The turtle went into the jungle to find the elephant. "Elephant, my friend, I am here to visit," said the turtle. "You're not my friend," said the elephant. "You're too small and weak to be my friend." "Elephant, don't get angry," said the turtle. "Let's meet tomorrow and have a test of strength—a tug-of-war. We will both tug at the ends of a vine. If I move you, I am the stronger. If you move me, then you are the stronger. If neither of us moves, we will be equal and we will be friends."

The elephant thought the test was silly but agreed. So the turtle got a very, very long vine and gave the elephant one end. "Tomorrow, when you feel the vine shake, we will start pulling and neither sleep nor eat until the test ends," said the turtle.

Then the turtle went to see the hippo and the same thing happened. The hippo did not want to be called the turtle's friend but agreed to the tug-of-war. He took the other end of the very, very long vine.

Early the next day, the turtle went to the middle of the vine and shook it. The elephant grabbed his end and the hippo grabbed his end, and the tugging began. Each pulled at the vine with all his strength, and it remained tight. At times, it moved a little toward the hippo and then a little toward the elephant, but neither one could pull the other very far.

The turtle watched the tightened vine. Then he went away to look for food, leaving the two at their contest.

Late in the afternoon, after eating and resting, he rose and said, "I will go and see whether those fools are still pulling." When he got back, the vine was still stretched tight with neither of them winning. At last, the turtle cut the vine. The vine snapped and at their ends, the elephant and the hippo fell with a great crash back onto the ground.

The turtle started off with one end of the broken vine. He came to the elephant who was looking sad and rubbing a sore leg. The elephant said, "Turtle, I did not know you were so strong. When the vine broke, I fell over and hurt my leg. Yes, we are really equals. Strength is not because the body is large. From now on, we will call each other friend."

Most pleased with this victory over the elephant, the turtle then went off to visit the hippo, who looked sick and was rubbing his head. The hippo said, "So, Turtle, we are equal. We pulled and pulled and even with my great size, I could not win. When the vine broke, I fell and hurt my head. Indeed, you are certainly as strong as I am. We will call each other friend."

After that, whenever these three got together with others, the three sat together on the highest seats. And always they addressed each other as friend.

Do you think they were really equal?

DISCUSSION EVALUATION SHEET 2

By now, your class has probably made progress toward group formation and participation. It is hoped that students are talking directly to one another more often than not and most are participating in each discussion. In addition, students comments and opinions should mostly be related to the topic at hand. Before answering the questions below, review the last evaluation sheet to familiarize yourself with your group's previous progress.

Remember that these questions ask about goals that should already have been met as well as those that lie ahead. Do not worry if most of the goals are not met. Instead, use your answers as you plan future sessions. Some of these goals will be worked on throughout the year.

There are many possible reasons why a goal is unmet. Take, for example, the first question about participation. It may be that your class has a small number of members participating. Ask yourself why this is so. It may be because the large group discussions are just beginning to gather steam when time runs out, that a few students are dominating the discussion, that quieter students do not yet feel comfortable in the whole group, or that some students are uninterested in this activity. Each of these explanations will require a different approach from you as you try to increase participation.

Are the students expressing ideas relevant to the topic?
❏ Never ❏ Sometimes ❏ Often ❏ Always

Do nearly 75 percent of the students participate in the large group discussion?
❏ Yes ❏ No

Have all students participated in at least one discussion?
❏ Yes ❏ No

Are all the students participating in the small groups?
❏ Never ❏ Sometimes ❏ Often ❏ Always

Are the students speaking directly to one another?
❏ Never ❏ Sometimes ❏ Often ❏ Always

Lesson 8

Pandora's Box
A Tale from Greece

PURPOSE

Today's text addresses a topic with which we all have experience—curiosity. Students' task is to use their experience with curiosity to explore Pandora's actions in today's story.

Students will:
- Relate their own experience to the text by sharing incidents from their own lives that are similar to the incident in the myth.
- Elaborate on a situation that happened to them or someone they know in which unrestrained curiosity caused problems.
- Cooperate and use their collective experience to understand a text.

INTRODUCTION

All human beings are, in one respect, just like Pandora, the main character in today's text. As a species, we are intensely curious. We love to find out new pieces of information, although we pursue it in different ways—from investigating a scientific mystery or scholarly work to watching or reading the news to traveling the world or listening to gossip. From our earliest years of life, everyone talks about other people they know. Sometimes we do this to get information we need; other times we do it because we are simply curious. In fact, we can see this aspect of ourselves and how similar we are to Pandora when we remember that almost nothing stirs our interest like being told that a piece of information is being intentionally hidden from us or kept a secret.

Teachers rarely need to develop or instill curiosity in their students. Rather teachers have the difficult task of directing the students' natural curiosity into areas or subjects that are educationally appropriate. Sometimes the problem they

Lesson 8: Pandora's Box

face is that subject matters seem too alien to students' daily interests to engage their already existing curiosity. At other times, our students already believe they know an answer and become complacent. Another problem may be that some students fear the risk of failure or the possibility of change that always comes with learning something new. Each of these situations poses special problems for educators, and we all have different solutions. However, we cannot be present to focus our students' curiosity whenever they need us to in their lives. Therefore it is necessary to help them direct their own curiosity. Touchstones Discussions create an environment in which that is possible—one in which students begin to teach themselves.

One of the first steps in this process is to give the students practice in using their own experience and interests to become engaged with a text or a subject matter. Up to now, the Touchpebbles Texts have been used to provoke the students to reflect on the multiple perspectives their experience offers them. Today, the students will apply their own experiences in a directed effort to understand a text.

Lesson Summary

One of the great mythic tales of the world is the story of Pandora's box. It is a story about curiosity and the consequences that can ensue when we allow it to consume us.

The worksheet helps the students focus on this topic by asking them to explore what most provokes their curiosity. It begins by asking them to rank subjects, people, or types of events about which they are curious. In small groups, the students share their own stories of curiosity. After the students have explored the general issue of curiosity, read the story to them. You should begin the discussion by asking the students why Pandora's curiosity increased when she was forbidden to open the box. As the students begin to investigate this question, invite them to recount comparable situations from their own experience. For example, ask them why being told that something was none of their business made them even more eager to know about it.

Possible Questions to Raise

- Why does Pandora get even more curious when she is told not to open the box?
- Can you think of a time when curiosity created problems in your own life?
- Why are people curious?
- Is curiosity always bad? Why or why not?
- If you were in Pandora's place, would you have opened the box? Why or why not?

Lesson 8: Pandora's Box

LESSON PLAN 8

Activity   **Time**

1. ARRANGE CLASSROOM .... 5 min.
2. INDIVIDUAL WORK .... 5 min.
    - Have the students answer questions 1 and 2.
    - In preparation for the Small Group Work, ask them to think of (but not to write down) a story from their own lives in which curiosity led to trouble.
3. SMALL GROUP WORK .... 8 min.
    - Divide the class into groups of three to five students.
    - Ask group members to share their stories with one another.
4. TEXT .... 2 min.
    - Gather the students back into a large circle.
    - Read the text aloud while they read along silently.
5. DISCUSSION .... 20 min.
    - Ask the students why Pandora's curiosity increased when she was forbidden to open the box.
    - For the last five to ten minutes of class, invite the students to share anecdotes that show how curiosity can lead to problems.

Total: 40 minutes

TOUCHPEBBLES VOLUME A

Worksheet 8: Pandora's Box

INDIVIDUAL WORK

1. Do you get more curious when someone tells you not to be?

    ❏ Yes   ❏ No

2. We are all curious about different things. Circle the number below that best describes how curious these situations make you feel.

    1 = Very curious   2 = A bit curious   3 = Don't care

    a) I know my parents have hidden presents for me in the house.

        1   2   3

    b) My friend won't tell me a secret.

        1   2   3

    c) Someone I don't like won't tell me who is spreading a bad rumor about me.

        1   2   3

    d) My teacher shows me a book he or she thinks I should read.

        1   2   3

    e) I wonder how lost dogs find their way home.

        1   2   3

    f) I visit some place I've never been to before, and someone asks me if I'd like to explore it.

        1   2   3

SMALL GROUP WORK

Think of stories from your own lives in which curiosity led to trouble. Share your stories with one another.

Lesson 8: Pandora's Box

Pandora's Box
A Tale from Greece
(STUDENT VOLUME, PAGE 21)

Zeus, the most powerful of all the Greek gods, was still angry that the giant Prometheus had given the gift of fire to mankind. He was also angry with humans because of the new skills they developed with the help of the fire. So Zeus thought up a dreadful plan to get even. He created the first woman, who was to be given to Prometheus' brother, another giant whose name was Epimetheus. This first woman was made from clay on the mountain of Olympus, and she was very beautiful. All the gods and goddesses gave her something to make her even more perfect. One taught her to sing, another gave her the gift of speaking well, and yet another gave her the skill of getting along with others. Finally, Zeus gave her a beautiful golden box, but he told her that she must never open it. Then he sent her to Earth to be the wife of Epimetheus.

Epimetheus loved her as soon as he saw her and forgot that his brother had warned him never to accept a gift from Zeus. He asked the woman, whose name was Pandora, about the box, and she told him that she had been ordered never to open it. But she felt sure it contained something valuable and wonderful. "Let us open it together," she said to her husband. Epimetheus, however, also told her never to open it, for he feared what Zeus might have done.

But the more Pandora was told not to open it, the more she wondered about what was inside. She fought against the temptation for a long time. Then, one day, she gave in and said to herself, "If I just open it up a tiny bit, peep inside to see, and then close it quickly, no one will ever know except me."

She opened it just a little, but out rushed a dark cloud of ugly, buzzing insects that swarmed in all directions. There was no way Pandora could ever get them back inside. The great number of insects that spread all over the earth became the spirits of hatred, greed, pain, illness, and war—all the evils that have hurt mankind ever since.

But one last gift remained in the box. It was the spirit of hope. Pandora wondered whether that might be any use against all the evils she had let loose.

Lesson

The Confessions
by Saint Augustine of Hippo

PURPOSE

Lesson 9 offers an occasion for students to explore a topic similar to curiosity, which we explored in the previous lesson. Today's text addresses the temptation to do something that we know we shouldn't do. The wide experiences that your students have had with this kind of temptation makes this discussion a good one in which to focus on increasing the number of students participating in Touchpebbles.

Students will:
- Examine the temptation to do something that is against the rules.
- Generate ideas about the source of such a temptation.
- Relate their own experiences with the situation of temptation—and action—outlined in the text.

INTRODUCTION

In the previous lesson, your students considered why we enjoy learning secrets and why our natural curiosity increases when we are told that something is none of our business. Curiosity is a kind of thinking that leads to knowing and understanding. However, we not only think, we also act. Today's case is comparable to that of Pandora's box but has to do with action rather than knowledge. We are all familiar with the temptation to do something that is forbidden. The moment we are told not to do something, the act takes on a new and

> **BENCHMARK**
> Now that your students have completed several lessons, the discussions are beginning to stay on topic with less direction from you, although the students will continue to need help. There should also be fewer long one-on-one exchanges between students taking place in the discussion.

Lesson 9: The Confessions

sometimes irresistible appeal. The text addresses this temptation by examining a an instance of stealing.

Temptation is a topic with which all your students have had a great deal of experience. Although few of them have probably ever stolen anything, they have all disobeyed various authorities, including their parents and other relatives, teachers, and even the Touchpebbles ground rules. On this topic therefore, they are experts, and each student will have something to offer. Your awareness of each student's ability to contribute is important because it is likely that some of your students have not spoken in the large group discussion yet or have only participated in very small ways. Today's topic may be a good way to bring these silent students into the discussion.

It is not crucial that all students speak in every discussion nor is it possible for them to do so. What is important is that everyone is a potential speaker. No one student should always remain silent or always be speaking. Yet these behaviors have most likely been an issue in your group, and you will need to make an effort to modify them. Today's text is a helpful tool for balancing participation. It often happens that some students remain silent because they still view Touchpebbles Discussions as a required school activity and thus are as hostile to these discussions as they are to regular classes. Such behavior is ssimilar to that of Saint Augustine. You should realize that such students probably know more about the type of situation that Saint Augustine describes than do those students who generally speak in class and do not feel tempted to resist authority.

Lesson Summary

In this week's reading, Saint Augustine recounts an incident from his youth in which he and some friends stole pears. He tells us that he knew stealing was wrong and that he didn't even want what he stole. Yet, in spite of that, he derived pleasure from stealing. He enjoyed it precisely because it was forbidden. Although this is a complex feeling, it is one to which many students will relate. You shouldn't simplify this text into a clear-cut situation of right versus wrong. It is the very complexity of the situation that will give quiet students an opportunity to participate.

The worksheet will help you bring two different groups of students into the discussion. The first question asks for reasons that people would have for not stealing. This question will be the kind to which your "good" students generally volunteer answers. The second question is more difficult, since it involves acknowledging one's temptations. However, we have found that many students who don't freely participate in organized class activities are often the ones who are more forward in answering this question. You should therefore encourage them to share, even by asking them directly, what responses they gave. You should view this text as an occasion for increasing the number of participants in the discussion.

POSSIBLE QUESTIONS TO RAISE
- Why does the knowledge that stealing is wrong make the author want to do it?
- Why is it tempting to do things we aren't supposed to do?
- Can you think of a time when you were tempted to do something you knew was wrong?
- Would stealing be less wrong if the author had actually needed the thing he stole?

Lesson 9: The Confessions

LESSON PLAN 9

| Activity | Time |

Activity   **Time**

1. **ARRANGE CLASSROOM** .... 5 min.
2. **INDIVIDUAL WORK** .... 10 min.
   - Have the students answer questions 1 and 2.
   - Since the worksheet is rather long, you may wish to read the questions aloud and answer any questions the students may have about the instructions.
3. **SMALL GROUP WORK** .... 5 min.
   - Divide the class into groups of three to five students.
4. **GROUP REPORTS** .... 3 min.
   - Bring the students back into the large circle.
   - Ask them to volunteer their answers for one of the questions. When students stop volunteering, begin asking students directly what their responses were. Every student should report his or her answer to one of the two questions.
5. **TEXT** .... 2 min.
   - Read the text aloud while the students read silently.

6. **DISCUSSION** .... 15 min.
   - Point out that Saint Augustine says that he stole the pears because he was "simply doing something that was forbidden."
   - Ask the students what the author means by that and whether the statement seems true to them.
   - At some point, you might ask them which of the reasons given in question 2 might be closest to Saint Augustine's reason and why they think so.

Total: 40 minutes

Worksheet 9: The Confessions

INDIVIDUAL WORK

1. You, like almost all people, probably have felt tempted to take something that belongs to someone else. But you probably did not steal. Instead, you resisted the temptation to take something. Try to remember that feeling of wanting to take something and also the feeling of resisting or not actually taking it. Check one of the following statements that seems most true and check one statement that seems least true. Read all the choices before you decide and pick only one most-true statement and one least-true statement.

I do not steal because:	**Most true**	**Least true**
a) I know it's wrong.	❑	❑
b) Someone might see me.	❑	❑
c) Other people will not like me.	❑	❑
d) I might get punished.	❑	❑
e) I don't want others to steal from me.	❑	❑
f) It's against the law.	❑	❑

2. If doing something is wrong (like taking something that belongs to someone else) and people are told not to do it, why do some people feel very strongly that they want to do it anyway? Check the letters of those reasons that seem true to you.

   _____ a) When people see something they want, they feel like taking it.

   _____ b) It's exciting to do things that are wrong.

   _____ c) The more people are told not to do something, the more they want to do it.

   _____ d) It makes people feel smart to get away with it.

   _____ e) Their friends make them want to do it.

SMALL GROUP WORK

As a group, compare your answers to question 2. Were there any letters that everyone in your group circled? Were there any that no one circled?

Lesson 9: The Confessions

The Confessions
by Saint Augustine of Hippo
(STUDENT VOLUME, PAGE 23)

No thief, not even a rich one, will let another man, even one who is very poor, steal from him. This shows that everyone knows in their heart that stealing is wrong. Yet I both wanted to steal and did steal. And what is so surprising, I was not made to do it because I needed anything. I stole something that I already had. I stole pears, although I already had pears that were better than the ones I took. I had no wish to eat what I stole. What I enjoyed was the stealing itself.

Near my parents' garden was a neighbor's pear tree. Although it was loaded with pears, they looked rotten. Even so, some friends and I got the idea of shaking the pears off the tree and carrying them away. We set out late at night and stole all the fruit we could carry. We tasted a few and then threw the rest to the pigs. We took no pleasure in eating the pears nor in being out late at night. What we liked was simply doing something that was forbidden.

Lesson 10

Emile or On Education
by Jean Jacques Rousseau

PURPOSE

Previous classes have explored perspectives of many kinds. In other lessons, the students compared how they saw themselves with how others saw them. In Lesson 10, the exploration of perspective moves to a higher level.

Students will:
- Take on or imagine the perspective of a parent.
- Explore their own opinions on child-rearing.

INTRODUCTION

Taking on a perspective is one of the crucial skills that must be learned to teach oneself. This skill will be practiced throughout the rest of this volume. Often in discussions, we inaccurately hear what others say—that is, we hear what we want to hear or what we expect to hear. In addition, we rarely realize that some of our opinions may not be objectively correct but still are legitimate slants on events, issues, or people. In order to adequately grasp another person's point of view as well as fully understand one's own opinions, the ability to take on or imagining a perspective is pivotal. The activity requires us to delineate the differences and similarities between our own perspective and the one we are attempting to imagine, thus forcing us to see each position more clearly. Because we are so close to ourselves, we often imagine that other people are much more similar to us than they really are. We must therefore try to see ourselves more clearly. This clarity will make it possible to both understand others and evaluate our own beliefs, needs, and goals. The text by Rousseau and the worksheet will encourage your students to create a vantage point from which to view themselves.

Lesson 10: Emile or On Education

LESSON SUMMARY

Rousseau's text is about how children should be raised. It focuses on a danger every parent acknowledges: spoiling a child. Children are born helpless and dependent. From the start of their lives, parents take care of them. When they cry or ask for something, parents try to figure out what they need and supply it. Both child and parent develop a definite pattern of behavior, habit, and expectation. Rousseau's text focuses on the danger of allowing this early relationship to continue. The risk of doing so, he states, is raising a child who is spoiled. In one sense, it appears easier—both for us and for a child—not to change definite ways of behaving. In many ways, it seems easier to continue to give a child what he or she needs. However, Rousseau points out that, at some point, we will have to say no, and the moment we choose to do so is crucial. If we wait too long, the child will become spoiled—a tyrant who expects everything and becomes furious when we eventually have to refuse. When such a child enters the larger world, for example, school, other adults or other children react very differently from the child's parents. The result for the spoiled child is a great shock. The child becomes uncertain and afraid and feels very weak.

Many students in your class are still living through the transition from life at home to life at school. Some, in fact, may be "spoiled" children who are experiencing just what Rousseau describes. Even if they aren't spoiled, they likely have been warned against, or accused of, becoming spoiled. Therefore, they will have very definite ideas about spoiled children, although it is unlikely that any of them see themselves that way. The worksheet asks the students to list some of the characteristics of a spoiled child. By implication, this question will make them look at themselves. Then they are asked to imagine themselves as parents raising a child and to decide how they would treat the child to avoid spoiling him or her. However, the students are really being asked how they should have been and should now be treated. This activity encourages them to *take on* a perspective on themselves. They must look at themselves not merely as their peers view them but also as adults, parents, and teachers might view them. This is a crucial step of imagining because they have not had the experience of being an adult.

POSSIBLE QUESTIONS TO RAISE

- What should parents do to avoid spoiling their children?
- How do you know what you should give a child and what you shouldn't?
- Why does the author think that spoiling children makes them unhappy?
- What does the author mean when he says that spoiled children "believe they own the whole world"?
- How do children who aren't spoiled act?
- What does the author mean when he says that spoiled children feel very weak as they get older?

Lesson 10: Emile or On Education

LESSON PLAN 10

Activity	Time
1. ARRANGE CLASSROOM	3 min.
2. DISCUSSION, PART 1	8 min.

- Ask the students what people mean when they say someone is spoiled.
- Ask for a volunteer to give an answer, and then go around the circle until all the students have given an answer. Write their answers on the board.
- Allow the students to discuss their different answers, and then ask them to help you make another list, this time of things that spoiled children ask for the most.

3. TEXT .... 2 min.
- Read the text aloud and have the students read along silently.

4. INDIVIDUAL WORK .... 5 min.
- Pass out the worksheet.
- Have students complete the Individual Work.

5. SMALL GROUP WORK .... 5 min.
- Divide the class into groups of three to five students.
- Ask the group members to come to an agreement about the best way to avoid spoiling a child.

6. GROUP REPORTS .... 7 min.
- Reconvene the large group and have each small group share its consensus on the best way to treat children so they don't become spoiled.

7. DISCUSSION, PART 2 .... 10 min.
- Allow discussion to naturally flow from group reports, if possible. If not, begin the discussion by asking students why asking the students why spoiled children might be unhappy.

Total: 40 minutes

TOUCHPEBBLES VOLUME A

Lesson 10: Emile or On Education

Emile or On Education
by Jean Jacques Rousseau
(STUDENT VOLUME, PAGE 25)

Do you know the most likely way to make your children unhappy? You can make them unhappy by giving them everything they want. When it is so easy for them to get what they want, they want more and more things. They will want your hat, your watch, and even the birds in the air. So sooner or later, because you can't keep up with them, you will have to say no. This will cause more pain than if you had not tried to give them everything they had wanted. Such children believe they own the world. They think all people are their slaves. When you try to explain why you finally said no, they think it's just an excuse. They feel they have been wronged and hurt by you. They begin to hate everyone. They are never grateful. They never thank anyone.

Could such children ever be happy? No. They are tyrants. I have seen children raised this way fill the air with their cries the moment they are not obeyed. They complain all the time. They beat on the table. And what are they like when they grow up and go out into the world or start school? There, they are surprised when they don't get their own way. In the world, people don't jump to get them what they want. They thought everything was theirs, and now they can't understand what has happened. They become afraid and mixed up and begin to feel they are very weak. When they were younger, they felt they could do anything. Now, they feel they can do nothing. Nature has made children to be loved and helped. But should we fear and obey them?

Worksheet 10: Emile or On Education

INDIVIDUAL WORK

You probably know a spoiled child. You may have called someone spoiled. All the sentences below are true to some extent, but some are more true than others. Check the letter of the sentence that you think is the most true.

- ❏ a) A spoiled child expects others always to do what he or she wants.
- ❏ b) A spoiled child never considers other people's feelings.
- ❏ c) A spoiled child makes life miserable for everyone nearby.
- ❏ d) A spoiled child is selfish.
- ❏ e) A spoiled child never does what you ask.
- ❏ f) A spoiled child is never satisfied.

SMALL GROUP WORK

What is the best way to avoid spoiling children? Check the letter of the one that you agree is best, or write your own answer.

- ❏ a) You should punish them.
- ❏ b) You should feel sorry for them.
- ❏ c) You should ignore them.
- ❏ d) You should try to change their mind by talking to them.
- ❏ e) You should take away privileges or things they like.
- ❏ f) _____

Lesson 11

The Pillow
A Tale from the Middle East

PURPOSE

Today's lessons asks your students to examine the value of teaching as well as the value of learning from one another. One of the main goals of Touchpebbles is for your students to learn how to teach and how to learn from others.

Students will:
- Evaluate their willingness to accept advice and learn from others.
- Recognize the role others play in their education.

INTRODUCTION

As teachers, you know that teaching is never a simple or straightforward task. Often parents, and sometimes your students, imagine that teaching is a kind of one-directional activity. The teacher knows a piece of information, and the task is simply to place this information in the mind of the student, like moving a table from one room to another. Of course, stating the situation in such bald terms makes us immediately realize the inaccuracy of this characterization. Teaching is a highly complex activity in which both the student and the teacher must cooperate. The student must have a fairly accurate sense of what he or she needs to know and, of course, a desire to satisfy that need. The teacher must recognize what the student knows as well as what the student needs to learn. This awareness helps the teacher develop a strategy to help the students bridge from what is familiar to them to what is unknown. Your students can explore these student-teacher relations this week in the simple, familiar activity of giving advice.

Giving advice is a type of teaching that all your students have experienced. They all have certainly received advice and probably most or all have at one time or another attempted to give it. It is useful to view teaching through the model of

Lesson 11: The Pillow

giving advice because the activity involves both the adviser and the advisee. Although giving advice sometimes succeeds, more frequently it fails. The reasons for its failure bring out the issues involved in all teaching. Sometimes giving advice fails because a person doesn't realize he or she needs advice, and therefore it becomes a difficult and often insurmountable task to get advice across. However, even if people recognize that they need advice, they can still resist accepting it. Sometimes people will only accept advice when they ask for it and then only from particular people. If advice is offered without being asked for, it is frequently refused. It would be useful to have the group discuss why. Sometimes even when it is asked for from a particular person, the advice is still not taken. This can occur because the adviser does not know how to present the advice so that it makes sense to the other person's perspective. These issues will be brought up in the worksheet exercises and the text.

Lesson Summary

This week's text is a story about two men who meet at an inn. The younger man begins to complain about his life and that he is poor and must work long hours; the older man tries unsuccessfully to get him to stop complaining. He gives the young man a magic pillow. While the young man sleeps, he dreams that he has been given what he has been asking for—wealth, power, and position—but also that possessing what he has wished for has put his life in jeopardy. The dream is so vivid that he feels that it is really happening. This experience makes him change his mind. Thus, the dream proves to be a successful piece of advice. The question arises, How could the old man have accomplished what the dream was able to achieve?

The worksheet brings up the same issue by making the students take on both perspectives, as advisees and as advisers. Other issues that the story raises are whether the difference in age prevents the young man from accepting the old man's advice and whether the young man knows that the old man spoke into the pillow so as to influence the dream. The latter seems possible because the young man thanks the old man for the pillow and the advice. The successful strategy in the story seems to be that one can help advisees accept advice by making them feel the consequences of what they plan to do. This tactic acknowledges that people tend not to accept advice that contradicts what they want. You might encourage the students to suggest and explore different strategies for giving advice. Two possible strategies are (a) raising cases of people in similar situations who have come to regret acting as they once wished and (b) listening hard and trying to decide what someone really wants and to explain how one does or doesn't achieve it. There are, of course, other routes that your students might suggest.

Possible Questions to Raise

- Why wouldn't the young man take the old man's advice at the beginning?
- Why does the young man change his mind?
- Do you think it is easier to give advice or to take it? Why?

- How can you tell the difference between good and bad advice?
- What would make you ignore someone's advice?
- Why do people sometimes ignore good advice?

Lesson 11: The Pillow

LESSON PLAN 11

| Activity | Time |

1. **ARRANGE CLASSROOM** .... 3 min.
    - Ask your students to sit in a circle.
2. **INDIVIDUAL WORK** .... 7 min.
    - Pass out the worksheet.
    - Ask the students to answer questions 1 and 2 individually. Help them by reading the questions aloud and clarifying any misunderstandings.
3. **SMALL GROUP WORK** .... 10 min.
    - Divide the class into groups of three to five students and ask them to share with one another their answers to question 1 in the Individual Work.
    - With their own preferences in mind, have them discuss which strategy in question 2 in the Individual Work will work the best to overcome the kinds of resistance they have expressed in answering question 1.
    - Encourage the small groups to agree on a strategy and to provide reasons why that strategy would be best.
4. **TEXT** .... 2 min.
    - Read the story aloud while the students read along silently.
5. **DISCUSSION** .... 18 min.
    - At some point, you may point out to them that the old man probably talks into the hollow glass pillow to influence the young man. Ask the students why the young man isn't angry at being fooled, and whether the young man knows the old man is talking into the pillow.

Total: 40 minutes

Worksheet 11: The Pillow

INDIVIDUAL WORK

1. Why do you sometimes not listen to someone who is trying to help you decide what to do? Check two of the following possibilities:

    ❏ You're too sure you are right.

    ❏ You want what you want too much.

    ❏ You don't like people telling you what to do.

    ❏ You only listen to one or two very close friends your own age.

    ❏ You only listen to older people.

    ❏ You don't like to admit you're wrong.

    ❏ (Other)_____

2. It's hard to accept even very good advice, especially if we want to do the opposite of what the advice suggests. Suppose your friend is angry with someone and wants to get even. You believe it's wrong, but your friend is too mad to listen. How would you get your friend to listen? Check the two strategies that you think are best.

    ❏ Keep repeating your opinion.

    ❏ Tell a story about the bad things that happened to someone else who did as your friend plans to do.

    ❏ Tell your friend you won't be his or her friend if he or she doesn't listen to you.

    ❏ Take your friend to three or four more people who agree with you.

    ❏ Talk with your friend until he or she calms down.

    ❏ (Other)_____

SMALL GROUP WORK

1. Share your answers to question 1 in the Individual Work with one another.
2. Choose an example in question 2 in the Individual Work that you think would help solve one of the possibilities you selected in question 1.
3. Decide as a group which strategy would work best.

The Pillow
A Tale from the Middle East
(STUDENT VOLUME, PAGE 27)

An old wise man stopped at an inn for the night. He was dressed simply and carried one bag in which were some books and a few clothes. Soon, a young farm worker came in wearing ragged clothes and sat beside the wise man. They began talking and telling each other stories and laughing. But then the young man started grumbling and saying how poor he was. He became sad telling how he was always hungry and unhappy and had no hope of making his life better.

"You look healthy and strong to me," said the old man. "Why complain now after you were laughing and content just five minutes ago?"

"I have to work hard from sunrise to sundown," said the young farm worker. "I should be a great general or a wealthy businessman or a popular singer. That way people would see how important I am."

When they were both tired and ready for bed and sleep, the wise man offered the youngster a pillow and said, "This is a special pillow that will grant all your wishes if you sleep on it." It was a strange pillow, for it was made of blue glass and was hollow inside and open at both ends. The young man eagerly took it and laid himself down and went to sleep. In no time at all the following things happened to him. He married a beautiful girl, he made a lot of money, he bought more and more land, and he made more money. He became so important that he was appointed chief adviser to the king. Then one day, a crafty assistant to the king accused him of stealing from the king and then lying about it. He pleaded that he was innocent, but the king sentenced him to die. Just as the sword was raised to cut off his head, he woke up. He was still at the inn. The wise man was lying beside him with his head by one end of the magic pillow. The innkeeper was cooking breakfast.

The young man was still shaking at breakfast and ate his food without speaking. When he had finished, he went to the wise man and kneeled humbly before him and said, "Thank you for the pillow, sir, and for the lesson you taught me. Now I know better how I should live well!"

Lesson 11: The Pillow

 DISCUSSION EVALUATION SHEET 3

As we near the halfway mark of the volume, participation is still increasing. The students should also be more and more self-guided in the small group work and in the discussions. Their participation should progress from talking to more cooperative aspects like paying attention to the speaker and speaking to all members of the group rather than through you or to a certain few others. The students must move from simply participating to participating responsibly and respectfully. In other words, the students must now move from simply participating to participating responsibly and respectfully.

This is not to say that all the previous goals have been met by all students but rather that the discussions are moving toward getting the students to work more cooperatively.

Are nearly all the students participating in each discussion?
❏ Never ❏ Sometimes ❏ Often ❏ Always

Are the small groups working efficiently?
❏ Never ❏ Sometimes ❏ Often ❏ Always

Are the students talking directly to one another and not through you?
❏ Never ❏ Sometimes ❏ Often ❏ Always

Are the students focusing their attention on the speaker?
❏ Never ❏ Sometimes ❏ Often ❏ Always

Are the students generating their own ideas about the topic?
❏ Never ❏ Sometimes ❏ Often ❏ Always

Are there a lot of arguments?
❏ Yes ❏ No

Are the discussions staying on topic?
❏ Yes ❏ No

Lesson

Catching Fish in the Forest
A Tale from Russia

PURPOSE

In the previous lesson, your students learned the value of learning from others. Today's lesson will explore the idea that information we receive from others is not always truthful or correct.

Students will:
- Read a story in which one person has been deceived by information and evidence from another individual.
- Examine the role evidence plays in our willingness to accept another person's point of view.
- Explore how we ultimately come to adopt another person's point of view.

INTRODUCTION

We all depend on others for various kinds of assistance in our daily lives. Nowhere is this more conspicuous than in our need for information. Since none of us can know everything, each of us must find ways to uncover the information we need. Therefore, we all must learn to evaluate and assess the continuous barrage of facts that pour in on us from friends, adults, and the media. A very astute grammar school teacher once said, "The truly intelligent person is not one who knows everything but one who knows where to go to find out. That's what we should be teaching." One place

> **BENCHMARK**
> Small group work is staying on task with less oversight from you. Students are also speaking more and more to the group as a whole.

Lesson 12: Catching Fish in the Forest

where students can begin to learn how to navigate the many sources of information available to them is in Touchpebbles Discussions. Students generally receive information from two routes, neither of which readily permits them to seriously assess what they are told. The formal route is from teachers. Teachers are believed because they are generally trusted, not because the students have evaluated the evidence for what teachers tell them. The second route is from informal sources outside school and from other learning situations. Information from these sources is believed or not believed on the basis of the attitude of the children involved, not because they have assessed what they have heard. Both formal and informal sources of learning are essential, but it is equally essential that the students learn to evaluate evidence and think for themselves. They can learn this skill in Touchpebbles Discussions because the Touchstones Method occupies an intermediate position between the two sources of learning. It is a formal learning situation, but one in which all contributors are roughly equal. Because the setting lacks an authority, an expert, and ties of friendship among the students, the students come to expect evidence for what people say.

Typically, we use certain criteria to assess evidence. For example, in the early seventeenth century, René Descartes suggested that we should doubt everything we hear or read and undertake to prove something to ourselves before we believe it. Fortunately Descartes is probably the only person ever to have tried this approach. Our general attitude is that we believe what we hear unless we have some reason to doubt it. In normal cases, our reasons for doubt can be of two sorts. Either we doubt the person who supplies the information, even if what he or she tells us is quite ordinary and unsurprising, or we trust the informant, even if what he or she tells us does not easily fit with all the other information we have previously accepted. However, in either situation, we may ultimately decide on the basis of evidence to accept the piece of information. The worksheet and text will focus the students on these issues of evidence.

Lesson Summary

Through the worksheet activities, the students look at a report of a very unusual event from two perspectives. In the first situation the students see something with their own eyes, but no one believes them. They are asked to select how they would respond. In the second situation, a friend tells them something that they find unbelievable, and they must choose a response. The small group work asks the students to consider the weight they would attach to the same report told by different people, including a parent, a sibling, a friend, or a stranger.

The text unites the two issues. A farmer who finds some treasure knows that his wife will tell everyone about it. He therefore decides to influence how people will take what she says. This is the strategy lawyers employ when they diminish the credibility of a hostile witness. In the story, the farmer creates a fantastic or unbelievable situation that he then has his wife observe. When she accurately reports what she has seen, everyone is so surprised by what she claims (namely, that it rained cookies and a rabbit was caught in a river) that they believe her husband when he tells everyone that she is crazy. Even though she tells the truth, what she sees so disagrees with everyone else's experience that they conclude that something is wrong with her. You might invite the students to bring up instances in which they were surprised at a piece of information but later came to believe it. They should discuss why they changed their mind.

POSSIBLE QUESTIONS TO RAISE

- Why do you think the duke did not believe the farmer's wife even though she told the truth?
- Do you think the farmer's wife could have convinced the duke to believe her story? How?
- Why do you think the duke believed the farmer's wife's first story but not the second one?
- Have you ever seen something and told someone else, but he or she did not believe you?
- Do you think that if the duke were to tell the story about the cookies in the tree, he would be able to convince others that the story was true?
- If a stranger and your best friend try to tell you something, whom would you believe first? Why?

Lesson 12: Catching Fish in the Forest

LESSON PLAN 12

| Activity | Time |

1. ARRANGE CLASSROOM .... 3 min.

2. INDIVIDUAL WORK .... 8 min.
- Pass out the worksheet and ask the students to answer both questions.

3. SMALL GROUP WORK .... 10 min.
- Divide the class into small groups and have them discuss their responses to the questions in the Individual Work.
- Ask the students whose account of something amazing they would most readily believe: a parent's, a sibling's, a friend's, or a stranger's, and why. It may help if the students can relate stories of not believing something and then changing their minds. What changed their minds?

4. TEXT .... 3 min.
- Call all the students back into the circle.
- Read the story aloud while students read along silently.

5. DISCUSSION .... 16 min.
- Ask the groups to share any stories they came up with in which people were initially surprised but later came to believe something unusual.

Total: 40 minutes

Worksheet 12: Catching Fish in the Forest

INDIVIDUAL WORK

1. You have seen something with your own eyes that is amazing. When you tell your friends, they think you're making it up. How do you react when they won't believe you? Check one.

    ❏ Tell the story again.

    ❏ Try to think of similar things they have seen and believed.

    ❏ Explain what you saw in more and more detail.

    ❏ Quietly walk away.

    ❏ Ask them to trust you.

    ❏ (Write some other reaction here)_____

2. A friend tells you something you just can't believe. He or she tells you he or she isn't fooling you, that it's really true, and that you must trust him or her. Yet it is still too hard to believe. What do you do? Check one.

    ❏ Ask for more details to see whether your friend changes any part of the story.

    ❏ Keep trying to get him or her to admit he or she is making it up.

    ❏ Ask other people you trust what they think and then agree with whatever they say.

    ❏ Believe your friend even though it's unbelievable.

    ❏ Refuse to talk about it anymore and continue to believe it's not true.

    ❏ (Write some other reaction here)_____

SMALL GROUP WORK

1. Discuss your responses from questions 1 and 2 in the Individual Work with the others in your group.
2. As a group, answer the following question:

   Whose account of something amazing would you believe most—a parent's, a brother's, a sister's, a friend's, or a stranger's? Why?

Lesson 12: Catching Fish in the Forest

Catching Fish in the Forest
A Tale from Russia
(STUDENT VOLUME, PAGE 29)

One day, a farm worker was digging in a field and found a large box of treasure. He took it home and said to his wife, "Look what I found. Where can we hide it?" They decided to bury it in the dirt floor. But then the man thought to himself, "My wife can't keep secrets. Soon the whole village will know about the treasure box." So he dug it up and buried it again behind the chicken coop. Then he went out and bought some oatmeal cookies and some fish, and he caught and killed a rabbit.

Very early the next morning, he quietly went out of their hut and left the fish on different paths in the forest. He threw the cookies up into the trees, and he tied the dead rabbit to a line that he dropped into the river. Later that morning, he said to his wife, "Please come with me into the forest and help me catch fish on the footpath for our dinner tonight."

She was amazed and cried out, "Fish in the forest?"

"Yes," he said. "I'm told there are several biting there today." So they went into the forest.

Very soon, she found a codfish on the footpath, then other small fish nearby. She couldn't believe her eyes, but she picked up the fish and put them in her basket. She looked up, and there on an oak tree's branches she saw some cookies, and over there some more cookies in a maple tree, and yet more in an elm tree. She showed her husband, and he said, "I must look to see whether I caught a rabbit in my trap." So he pulled the fishing line from the river, and there was the dead rabbit. "This is unbelievable!" she cried. But she added the rabbit to the fish and cookies in her basket, and when they returned home, she cooked a fine meal.

A week later, the man was told to come to the duke's palace. He knew the secret of his buried treasure had been told to people by his wife and that the duke had heard about it. Sure enough, the duke asked him, "Did you find some treasure and bury it in your house?" "No," replied the man. The duke said, "But your wife has been telling everyone that you did." "Oh, she's crazy," said the man. "She sees things that are not there. Just a few days ago she told me she had caught fish in the forest and a rabbit in the river and found cookies in the trees."

So the duke called for the farmer's wife and asked her whether her story about the treasure was true and when it had happened. "Of course it's true," she said. "It happened the day before I caught fish in the forest; in fact, the night before that, it had rained cookies. My husband caught a rabbit in the river with a fishing line the same day, too."

Now the duke knew the woman was crazy, and the man kept the treasure he had found.

Lesson 13

The Eagle
by Alfred, Lord Tennyson

PURPOSE
Lesson 13—the first Touchpebbles lesson using a poem—explores language and the many ways it can be used to express thoughts and images.

Students will:
- Evaluate three short passages and determine what makes them different from one another.
- Examine two passages about the same scene.
- Help one another comprehend an unfamiliar and abstract poem.

INTRODUCTION
Language serves many different purposes. For example, we can use it to meet the needs of different audiences, to describe a situation clearly, or to make a situation seem more or less dramatic. It is very important for a discussion group, which operates through language, to explore these different uses of language. In this week's lesson, the students will consider three different accounts of the flight of an eagle. One of these accounts is a poem by Tennyson; the other two are prose. The class will consider the differences and similarities of the three versions.

LESSON SUMMARY
Tennyson's poem takes an straightforward event—an eagle flying off a cliff (expressed clearly in version 1) and uses language to create other images that convey a dynamic sense of what one might call the eagle's nature. Although full of drama and imagery, the poem will seem inaccessible to most of your students, both because of its vocabulary ("azure world") and its images. What does it mean, for example, to say that an eagle has "crooked hands"?

Lesson 13: The Eagle

The poem describes an eagle sitting high up in a clear blue sky, clutching a rocky cliff edge. The eagle perches so high up that the presumably large sea waves below look like wrinkles. Then the eagle suddenly plunges down from its perch, "like a thunderbolt." Version 2 preserves the dramatic tone of the poem but clarifies the scene by translating some of the words and simplifying the images. The poem, for example, never calls its subject an eagle (except in the title) and uses phrases, like "crooked hands," that make one think of a human rather than a bird. Version 1 is the least dramatic account and describes the scene clearly and plainly.

For this lesson's discussion, you will need to provide a great deal of guidance and even direct help. Define words or clarify images briefly as you see fit. The students will benefit from struggling to understand the poem and from beginning to appreciate the variety of uses one can make of language. To ensure that the students start with a clear picture, they begin by drawing what is described by version 1. In question 2 of the Individual Work, the students compare versions 1 and 2. After you read the poem, focus the students on listing what is different about it and how it could be drawn. Ask them how their original drawings should be changed. Discuss what they prefer about each account of the event, and why they prefer what they do.

In the discussion, you might encourage the students to indicate their preference for one of the versions and to give a reason. Many students will probably prefer version 1, which is short and clear. You might ask them whether there is anything from version 2 or the poem that think is important yet not present in version 1. How would they change version 1 to include what they think is missing? In the poem, the words in the two stanzas end in rhymes. In the first stanza, the final words are "hands," "lands," and "stands;" in the second they are "crawls," "walls," and "falls." You might ask them whether that adds anything important to their sense of what is happening.

This lesson will be quite different from others you have had. To answer questions and make suggestions, you will need to assume more of a directive role than usual in Touchpebbles. At this point in Touchpebbles your students have had quite a bit of experience with discussions intended to develop skills. This week's lesson will enable all of you to see how discussions can help in exploring content, but will require you and your students to change roles during the lesson. The students will need to use discussion to figure out what information they need from you and then use that information to further their own discussion.

POSSIBLE QUESTIONS TO RAISE

- How would you change the drawings to match the way the poem describes the scene?
- Which of the three readings is the most interesting to you? Why?
- How important is the title in understanding the poem?
- How is the poem different from the first two passages?
- Which of the three passages would you use to help you draw your picture? Why?

Lesson 13: The Eagle

LESSON PLAN 13

Activity	Time
1. ARRANGE CLASSROOM	3 min.
2. TEXT	4 min.

- Read the versions 1 and 2 aloud several times while the students read along silently.
- Encourage the students to ask any questions they may have about the words.

3. INDIVIDUAL WORK .... 8 min.
- Pass out the worksheet and ask the students to draw the scene described by version 1. Have the students share their drawings, looking for differences but not criticizing other students' drawings.
- Display one or two drawings that the class agrees represent all the elements of the scene best.
- Have the students answer questions 2 and 3.

4. TEXT .... 3 min.
- Read the poem aloud at least twice while the students read along silently. Emphasize the rhyme scheme.

5. SMALL GROUP WORK .... 10 min.
- Divide the class into groups of four or five students.
- Have the students discuss what new details the poem adds.
- Have the groups make two lists (one student should volunteer to compile the lists): one of words they don't understand and the other of what they prefer about each version.

6. DISCUSSION .... 12 min.
- Have the students form the large circle again.
- Have the small groups report on their preferences.

Total: 40 minutes

TOUCHPEBBLES VOLUME A

Lesson 13: The Eagle

The Eagle
by Alfred, Lord Tennyson
(STUDENT VOLUME, PAGE 33)

Version 1

The eagle stands by himself on the top of the cliff high up in the sky. The sun shines in the blue sky. He looks at the sea waves below and flies down.

Version 2

High up in the sky, the lone eagle grips an edge of the rocky cliff with his claws. The bright sun shines down from a clear blue sky. He gazes down on the sea below, which is lightly ruffled by the wind. Suddenly, he swoops down.

The Eagle

by Alfred, Lord Tennyson

He clasps the crag with crooked hands;
Close to the sun in lonely lands,
Ringed with the azure world, he stands.

The wrinkled sea beneath him crawls;
He watches from his mountain walls,
And like a thunderbolt he falls.

Worksheet 13: The Eagle

INDIVIDUAL WORK

1. On the back of the worksheet, draw what you think is being described in version 1.

2. Versions 1 and 2 have many differences. Two differences are listed below. Make a "✔" for the one you prefer.

   a) Which do you prefer?

   ❏ The lone eagle   or   ❏ The eagle stands by himself

   b) Which do you prefer?

   ❏ He gazes down   or   ❏ He looks at

3. Write one more difference in describing the same thing that you can find between version 1 and version 2.

   From version 1. _____

   From version 2. _____

SMALL GROUP WORK

1. As a group, discuss what new details the poem adds.
2. Make two lists: one list of the words you don't understand and one list of what the group prefers about each version. Pick one person out of your group to write down the lists.

TOUCHPEBBLES VOLUME A

Lesson 14

They Share the Work
A Tale from Latvia

PURPOSE

In Lesson 13, your students learned that a single situation can be described in many ways. In Lesson 14, your students will discuss the importance of saying what they mean as clearly as possible.

Students will:
- Apply their personal experience to the ideas in the text to better understand its meaning.
- Understand the purpose and value of saying what one means.

INTRODUCTION

It is not uncommon for us to say things we don't mean. When we ask someone at dinner, "Can you pass the salt?" few companions would reply, "Yes, I can" and do nothing. We all recognize that the question wasn't whether the other person is *able* to pass the salt. Instead, the questioner wanted the other person to pass the salt. Similarly we recognize that when someone threatens, "If you do that, I'll never speak to you again," they generally don't mean it.

In law, this distinction between words and their meanings is described as the spirit versus the letter of the law. Children, like lawyers and their clients, use, and sometimes abuse, this distinction, when they want to "get around" a parental rule. For example, children may cleverly obey exactly what their parents say, while clearly violating parents' intention.

Lesson 14: They Share the Work

LESSON SUMMARY

The text for today's lesson examines the tension between what is said and what is meant. In the text, an industrious man sows a field with wheat and uses the grain to make flour for bread. A lazy man makes a deal with the first man for half of next year's crop. However, the lazy man agrees to collect everything that grows above ground. The worker decides to plant potatoes, thus getting all the food while the lazy man comes away with the worthless potato vines.

Clearly, the lazy man was trying to trick the other into giving him free food; but it is not clear whether the industrious man chose to plant potatoes to outwit the lazy man. Regardless, the lazy man did not get the deal he wanted because he didn't say what he meant, which was that he wanted half of the edible crop. It is not clear, however, that the worker would have made a deal at all if the lazy man had said what he really wanted.

The worksheet should be completed before the story is read. It specifically addresses the difference between what is actually said and what the speaker almost certainly intends. Based on a hypothetical instruction from a parent or guardian, the students must judge the appropriateness of three different actions. After they have judged the actions and discussed their judgments in small groups, you should read the story to them. In the large group discussion, the students should try to answer the last question of the story, Which one of them was good and honest? If a person can say, "I gave you exactly what you asked for," does that always make the person honest?

POSSIBLE QUESTIONS TO RAISE

- Ask your students to answer the last line of the story. Which of the two men was good and honest? Why?
- Have you ever tried to trick someone by saying something that wasn't exactly what you meant?
- How can we prevent misunderstandings like the one in the story?
- How can you make sure to say exactly what you mean?
- How do you know when someone is not being truthful?
- Can you think of any similar misunderstandings we have had in our discussions?

Lesson 14: They Share the Work

LESSON PLAN 14

Activity	Time
1. ARRANGE CLASSROOM	3 min.
2. INDIVIDUAL WORK	8 min.

- Pass out the worksheet.
- Read the instructions to the students and make sure that they understand how to complete the Individual Work.

3. SMALL GROUP WORK . . . . 15 min.

- Divide the class into groups of four or five students and ask them to discuss their answers to the Individual Work and, if possible agree on the response for each question.
- Have the students share any personal stories they have of someone who obeyed the letter but not the spirit of someone else's words.

4. TEXT . . . . 2 min.

- Have the students form the large circle again.
- Read the story aloud while the students read along silently.

5. DISCUSSION . . . . 12 min.

- Ask the students to answer the question at the end of the story. You may wish to go around the circle and ask for volunteers. You should answer too, but do not begin or end with yourself.

Total: 40 minutes

TOUCHPEBBLES VOLUME A

Worksheet 14: They Share the Work

INDIVIDUAL WORK

Your parent or guardian tells you to take the shortest way home. You understand that your parent or guardian means that you're not supposed to play with your friends and get home late. Read the following three possible actions, and check all the words that you think describe your behavior.

a) If you come directly home by the shortest way without playing, you are being:

❑ obedient   ❑ disobedient   ❑ honest   ❑ tricky

b) If you take the shortest way but play with friends on the way home and get home late, you are being:

❑ obedient   ❑ disobedient   ❑ honest   ❑ tricky

c) If you take a longer way with friends but make sure you are home on time, you are being:

❑ obedient   ❑ disobedient   ❑ honest   ❑ tricky

SMALL GROUP WORK

1. Discuss your answers to the Individual Work with one another.
2. Try to agree to on a group response for each action above. If you cannot agree on answers for all three, then agree on one.

They Share the Work
A Tale from Latvia
(STUDENT VOLUME, PAGE 35)

Once there was a time when only two men lived in the world. One was good and honest, the other selfish and mean.

In the spring, one of the men dug in a field and planted wheat. The other man watched him doing this and was very puzzled. He watched day after day. As summer came with its rain and sun, the grain grew tall above the ground. In the fall, the first man cut the ripe wheat and made it into flour. Then he baked bread. He used his plow to make the soil better by mixing the roots of the wheat into the earth.

The next year, the second man went to the first and said, "Let's work together and share the crop. I'll take the part above the soil. You will have what's under the ground." The first man agreed, but this time he planted potatoes. In the fall, the first man kept the potatoes that were under the earth and had them to eat all winter. The second man had the worthless green tops that appear above the ground and was hungry all winter. He became angry and went to the first man to tell him he had been cheated. But the first man replied, "Why are you so angry with me? I gave you exactly what you asked for."

Which one of them was good and honest?

Lesson 15

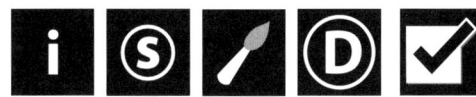

Two Portraits:
Portrait of a Clergyman
by Albrecht Dürer
Marchesa Brigida Spinola Doria
by Peter Paul Rubens

PURPOSE

In this lesson, your students will concentrate on perspective and how their perspective affects the way they evaluate other people and the world around them.

Students will:
- Compare two paintings and evaluate the artists' focuses.
- Recognize the uniqueness of students' perspective.
- Examine how the whole (i.e., the context) and particulars (i.e., the characteristics) influence our evaluation of what we see.

BENCHMARK
Students are beginning, as part of taking ownership, to routinely ask their own questions instead of expecting all the questions to be supplied for them. Often, students don't realize that this practice is acceptable and will need encouragement. They are also better able to control their participation and are interrupting one another less.

INTRODUCTION

When someone analyzes details too closely and misses the big picture, we sometimes say that he or she has failed to see the forest for the trees. Conversely, when someone sees only the big picture at the expense of important details, we can say that he or she failed to see the trees for the forest. Together, the expressions illustrate the importance of achieving a balanced perspective that includes evaluating the parts as well as the whole—a Touchpebbles goal.

Consider an example from music. In an orchestra or band, each member must be skilled at playing his or her instrument well and also skilled at playing together with other instrumentalist. The orchestra is unified by a conductor who knows the part played by each instrument and how the parts combine to form a whole piece of music. The bandleader has a dual role as a conductor and player.

In your Touchpebbles Discussions, your role so far has probably been most similar to that of an orchestra conductor, but it is likely moving toward the role of bandleader. Ultimately the goal of Touchpebbles is for your and your students' roles to be similar to the roles of members of a jazz band—musicians that play together without a single leader. Your Touchpebbles students must eventually learn how to be both participants and leaders. Not only is this skill needed for true discussion, it is necessary for students' futures in which they must develop concrete professional skills as well as recognize how their skills interrelate with those of others. They must be able to see both the trees and the forest.

Lesson Summary

This week's lesson, which uses portraits by Rubens and Dürer, will help students explore the relationships of parts and wholes. The students begin by completing the worksheet, which asks them what characteristics they find most helpful in judging someone they are meeting for the first time. For instance, do they look at the eyes or skin, or do they consider the person's body language, demeanor, or clothes? The worksheet also allows the students to suggest other factors, such as a person's voice, how he or she speaks, or his or her background or family.

Together, the portraits help students further explore the interplay of parts and wholes. The Dürer portrait focuses on a face, without much concern for the subject's location or clothing. By contrast, the Rubens portrait appears to give equal importance to the marchesa's face, how she stands, what she wears, and where she is. The Dürer portrait presents a person without a context whereas in the Rubens painting, the context is as important as the face. In having students consider whether one is a more successful portrait than the other, focus their attention on considering why each artist approached the subject as he did. Why might Dürer have focused his clergyman portrait on the man's eyes, lips, and mouth? Why might Rubens have thought the marchesa's surroundings were important to his portrait?

Help the students with words they don't know (a marchesa is like a princess, a clergyman is a pastor or priest). They will notice that the clothing is dated, but it's not necessary to make an issue of it. At some point in the discussion, you might bring up someone all the students have heard about and ask the students to discuss how to paint that person's portrait.

Lesson 15: Two Portraits

POSSIBLE QUESTIONS TO RAISE
- What are some of the main features of each painting?
- Which person would you like to talk with first? Why?
- What are the things you notice first in each of the paintings? Why do you think that is?
- What are the moods of the paintings? (i.e., Do you think the people are happy? Sad? Serious?)
- Have you ever met someone only once? If so, which do you remember first, his or her face or the place you met?
- Do the colors in the paintings determine how you feel about them? If so, how?

Lesson 15: Two Portraits

Lesson Plan 15

Activity   Time

1. **Arrange Classroom** .... 3 min.
2. **Individual Work** .... 7 min.
   - Pass out the worksheets, and have the students complete the Individual Work.
3. **Small Group Work** .... 10 min.
   - Divide the class into groups of four or five students and ask them to discuss their answers to the Individual Work. Suggest that they begin by taking turns saying what feature they find most useful and which elements they consider important in the photograph. Encourage them to give reasons for their answers.
4. **Paintings** .... 5 min.
   - Have students form the large circle, and show them the portraits.
5. **Discussion** .... 15 min.
   - First, ask the students to describe what they see in each portrait, and whether they like one better and if so, why. If time allows, mention one or two well-known people and ask how their portrait should be painted or how they should be photographed. Should the portrait or photograph focus on the face or the whole person in a setting?

Total: 40 minutes

Worksheet 15: Two Portraits

INDIVIDUAL WORK

1. If you want to find out as much as you can about a person just by looking at him or her, what are the best clues? Listed below are four clues you might find useful. Add one of your own ideas for item e, and then put the clues in order of usefulness or importance, with 1 meaning most useful and 5 meaning least useful.

    _____ a) skin (smooth, wrinkled, etc.)

    _____ b) eyes (big, drooping, bright, etc.)

    _____ c) how he or she stands or sits

    _____ d) the clothes he or she wears

    _____ e) My own idea of what to look at: _____

2. If you are taking a photograph of someone who you really want to remember, which of these would you do?

a) Focus on the face	❏ yes	❏ no
b) Photograph the whole person	❏ yes	❏ no
c) Have them look directly at you	❏ yes	❏ no
d) Have them look a bit to the side	❏ yes	❏ no
e) Have them stand in a place that is special to you both.	❏ yes	❏ no

3. For one of your "yes" answers, be able to give a reason.

SMALL GROUP WORK

Take turns sharing your answers from the Individual Work and discuss the differences.

**Two Portraits:
Portrait of a Clergyman**
by Albrecht Dürer

and

Marchesa Brigida Spinola Doria
by Peter Paul Rubens
(STUDENT VOLUME, PAGE 76)

The paintings for this lesson are located on page 234.

Lesson 15: Two Portraits

 DISCUSSION EVALUATION SHEET 4

This is the halfway point of this volume. Most of the students should be participating in a respectful manner. Although there are still likely arguments and other dynamics issues like dominance or certain students' remaining silent, on the whole, the discussions should be increasingly respectful and cooperative explorations.

As we look forward to developing listening and critical thinking skills, we are also looking forward to students' increased sense of ownership of the Touchpebbles Discussions. Students initiating their own lines of inquiry, working efficiently on individual and small group tasks, and following your directions are early indicators that they are sharing the responsibility for the discussions. Consequently, the time you spend talking and asking questions should be diminishing. Also, the students will begin to be concerned with their own participation. They will start to ask their own questions and be more concerned with being understood. You can assist them by asking them to give examples and explanations. Encourage the students to ask questions; our experience with elementary school students has been that they often do not realize that they are allowed to ask questions because they may not be expected to ask questions in other classes.

Are the small groups working efficiently?
❏ Never ❏ Sometimes ❏ Often ❏ Always

Are the students stating their ideas clearly?
❏ Never ❏ Sometimes ❏ Often ❏ Always

Are the students raising their own questions about the topic or the text?
❏ Never ❏ Sometimes ❏ Often ❏ Always

Are the students focusing their attention on the speaker?
❏ Never ❏ Sometimes ❏ Often ❏ Always

Do the students listen respectfully to one another?
❏ Never ❏ Sometimes ❏ Often ❏ Always

Are the students relating their experiences to the text?
❏ Never ❏ Sometimes ❏ Often ❏ Always

Lesson 16

The Republic
by Plato

PURPOSE

Lesson 16 asks students to examine the differences between their public behavior and their private behavior.

Students will:
- Examine a text in which a character becomes invisible.
- Discuss how their own behavior changes in public and private contexts.
- Investigate the causes of these different behaviors, and discuss whether the differences are always appropriate.

INTRODUCTION

How we behave when we are in public places like school can be very different from how we behave when we are alone, as in the privacy of our own home. Someone who dresses up for school may prefer more casual clothes at home. A child who is difficult at home may be well-behaved and agreeable in the classroom. In this lesson, the students will explore how they behave differently in private and in public. At first they may think of themselves as always the same, but upon reflection, all students will be able to relate experiences of changing their behavior to match the circumstances. For example, they may not even feel tempted to turn on the TV if a parent has forbidden it and is nearby, but the desire to turn it on may become overwhelming if that parent has to leave the house unexpectedly on a short errand.

The Touchpebbles Discussion itself can illustrate the range of challenges that people face in harmonizing their public and private behaviors. For example, in a public discussion, some students might feel pressure to say what they think others expect them to say. At the same time, other students might say exactly what they think, which may not always be appropriate. Part of the work of Touchpebbles is to

Lesson 16: The Republic

enable students to talk comfortably about substantive or controversial issues without making their comments so intensely personal or private that others are prevented from commenting.

Lesson Summary

In the text, Socrates suggests that people behave well primarily because they fear being seen—not because they are honest or well-behaved. He tells of a shepherd who discovers a magic ring that renders him not only invisible but also forgotten. The shepherd uses this power to commit many crimes and eventually overthrow the government. Socrates suggests that, given the ability to do what we want and not suffer any of the consequences of being seen, most people, perhaps all people, would not be honest and well-behaved. Your students may disagree with what Socrates suggests, and you should encourage them to bring up examples that would make Socrates reconsider his claim.

The worksheet asks the students to consider what they would or would not do while their parents are able to see them. Thus, the students can see how their own behavior is often changed by the mere condition of being seen by others. The reason that all Touchpebbles Discussions take place in a circle is so that all students can be seen. Being seen by everyone begins a long process that culminates in students taking responsibility for what they say and for what goes on in the discussions. How to speak in such a public way is an issue your students have been dealing with throughout the year.

Possible Questions to Raise

- If you were invisible, what would you do that you might not do when others can see you?
- What would you do if you had the ring?
- Do you speak differently in Touchpebbles Discussions than you do with your friends?
- Have these two ways of speaking become more or less similar to each other over the past few months?
- Why is our behavior in private situations different from how it is in public?
- When do you think you behave better: when you are in public or when you are in private? Why?
- Why do you think the man in the story used the ring to do harm instead of good?

Lesson 16: The Republic

LESSON PLAN 16

Activity	Time
1. ARRANGE CLASSROOM	3 min.

- Have the students sit in a circle.

2. TEXT . . . . 2 min.
- Read the story aloud while the students read along silently.
- Ask the students whether they would like to be invisible.

3. INDIVIDUAL WORK . . . . 8 min.
- Pass out the worksheet. Read it to the students, and make sure they understand how they are to answer both questions.

4. SMALL GROUP WORK . . . . 8 min.
- Divide the class into groups of four or five students, and ask them to compare their answers from the Individual Work. Was there one action that consistently received the same answer regardless of whether the parents could see it?

5. DISCUSSION . . . . 19 min.
- Have the students form the large circle again.
- Ask them how being invisible like the shepherd is like doing things in secret. How does the possibility of being seen affect our behavior?

Total: 40 minutes

TOUCHPEBBLES VOLUME A

Lesson 16: The Republic

The Republic
by Plato
(STUDENT VOLUME, PAGE 39)

Are people good because they want to be? Or are they good because they are afraid to be bad? To answer these questions, let us pretend we can give both the good and the bad person the freedom and power to do whatever he pleases. Then in our imaginations, we can see what he will do. I think the good person will be no different from the bad person, for he is really as selfish as the bad person. Only fear of the law makes him good. Let me tell you a story about a man who had such freedom.

People say that this man was a shepherd in the service of the king of Lydia. After a great rainstorm and an earthquake, the ground opened up where he was caring for the sheep, and he went into the opening in the earth. The story goes on to say that he saw many wonderful things there, among them a large bronze model of a horse with little doors on the side. When he looked in, he saw the body of a giant with a gold ring on its finger. He took the ring and left.

When the shepherds held their monthly meeting to report to the king about his flocks, the shepherd who fell into the earth also attended, wearing the ring. While he was sitting there twisting the ring on his finger, he happened to turn it so that the stone faced his palm. When he did this, the story goes on, he became invisible. Those who sat around him could no longer see him. They spoke about him as if he were not there. He was amazed and twisted his ring once more. When he turned the stone out, he became visible again. He tested this many times and found that the ring truly possessed the power to make him invisible. So with the help of this ring, he committed many crimes and took over the kingdom.

Now suppose we have two such rings. Let's give one to a good person and the other to an evil person. It is hard to believe that even a good man would stop himself from stealing and doing all kinds of other bad things if he knew he would never get caught.

Worksheet 16: The Republic

INDIVIDUAL WORK

1. Imagine that you are in a room in which your parents can see you, and mark a "✔" in the box that best describes your answer to the following questions.

   a) I'd watch TV before my homework was done.
      ❏ No   ❏ Maybe   ❏ Probably   ❏ Yes

   b) I'd eat candy instead of a healthy snack.
      ❏ No   ❏ Maybe   ❏ Probably   ❏ Yes

   c) I'd be very noisy.
      ❏ No   ❏ Maybe   ❏ Probably   ❏ Yes

   d) I'd tease someone.
      ❏ No   ❏ Maybe   ❏ Probably   ❏ Yes

   e) I wouldn't pick up after myself.
      ❏ No   ❏ Maybe   ❏ Probably   ❏ Yes

2. How would you answer the questions above if your parents could *not* see you? Mark an "✘" in the box for these answers in the examples above.

SMALL GROUP WORK

1. Compare your answers from the Individual Work.
2. Did the group agree on any of the answers? If so, which ones?

Lesson 17

How to Catch a Thief
A Tale from China

PURPOSE
In the previous lesson, the students considered how they behave or speak differently in public and private situations. In this lesson, they will consider the related issue of how to find out whether someone is telling us the truth.

Students will:
- Engage in an exercise in which the objective is to figure out whether someone is lying to them.
- Examine the strategies used in the exercise.
- Compare the strategies used in the exercise with a lie-detecting device used in today's story.

INTRODUCTION
It is often very frustrating to have to decide whether someone is telling the truth. In extreme situations, physical punishment is imposed, however it does not always yield the truth because people will often say whatever is necessary to end the punishment. Although asking questions is a more humane and appropriate route, that process can also be unreliable. Through skillful questioning, we can trap the other person into giving contradictory answers that may suggest the person is lying. The biggest obstacle to finding the truth may be the human tendency to hear only what we want to hear—no matter what the person does or says or what is true. Today's lesson will explore the difficulties of discerning the truth.

Lesson 17: How to Catch a Thief

Lesson Summary

The text tells the story of a wise judge who claims to be able to distinguish the truth from a lie without injuring or even questioning anyone. He says he has a bell that will ring when a thief touches it. Ultimately, one could say that his method involves an element of fear—the fear that the theft committed will cause the bell to ring and hence tell everyone of the person's guilt. Nevertheless, no physical harm takes place or is threatened.

However, before engaging in the large group discussion, the students should explore the issues in the text with a practical exercise. The worksheet tells the students to choose two facts about themselves: one is made-up but easily believable, the other is true but not easy to believe. In pairs, each student should tell his or her partner one of the two statements. The other person should try to figure out whether what he or she heard is true or made-up. In the large group, the students should discuss the difficulties they had in determining the truth of what they heard.

After discussing the exercise for a few minutes, the students should discuss whether the judge's method was a good one or whether the accused man was, in fact, truthful and honest.

Possible Questions to Raise

- Was it difficult to come up with your two statements?
- Which one was harder to come up with: a lie that is easy to believe or a true statement that is hard to believe?
- If you were parents, would you use the bell with your children?
- Would you be willing to let the bell be used on you?
- How is the bell different from a modern lie detector?
- Do you think the bell is a useful method? Does it work?
- How would you have approached the problem of finding the thief?

Lesson Plan 17

Activity	Time
1. Arrange Classroom	3 min.

- Ask the students to form a circle.

2. **Individual Work** .... 7 min.
   - Pass out the worksheet. Review the directions and make sure that the students understand what they are supposed to do.
   - Point out to the students that for the exercise to be challenging, the false statement should be easily believable and the true statement should seem unlikely. For instance, a student could say falsely that a famous singer is a relative or say truly that they once met a famous baseball player.
   - Give the students time to decide what to write. If you wish, go around the room and help each student.

3. **Pair Work** .... 10 min.
   - Pair together students who do not know each other well.
   - Have each student tell his or her partner one statement from the Individual Work.
   - The students must decide and say whether they think their partner's statement is true or false.
   - At the end of the exercise, have the students tell their partners whether they are correct.

4. **Pairs Reports** .... 5 min.
   - Have students form the large circle, and ask them what they liked or did not like about the exercise and whether it was difficult or easy.

5. **Text** .... 2 min.
   - Read the story aloud while students read along silently.

6. **Discussion** .... 13 min.
   - Begin the discussion by asking the students whether the king's method of lie detection is a good one.

Total: 40 minutes

Worksheet 17: How to Catch a Thief

 INDIVIDUAL WORK

Write two statements about yourself below. One should be true and the other false. Do not mark them as true or false or put them in any special order. Make the false statement something about you that someone could believe and the true statement something about you that people in your class might find hard to believe.

1.

2.

 PAIR WORK

1. Choose one of your statements. Do not tell your partner whether it is true or false.
2. Read your statement aloud to your partner, and listen to your partner's statement. Decide whether your partner's statement is true or false, and circle your choice below. You cannot ask your partner any questions to figure out whether he or she is telling the truth.

   My partner's statement is: True   False

How to Catch a Thief
A Tale from China
(STUDENT VOLUME, PAGE 41)

Many years ago a wise judge lived in a small village. People came to him from the whole country to get his help. It was said he could solve a crime without ever questioning a suspect or without hurting or torturing a person until he or she confessed. He believed both those ways of getting information were not really useful. If you hurt someone, that person will often say whatever is needed to get you to stop. If you question someone, you often hear what you want the suspect to say. Therefore, the judge always looked for ways to trap a suspect so that he could be sure to solve the crime.

One day a great king and all his assistants came to him. The king knew that one of them had stolen a valuable jewel, but the king and all his wise men could not figure out which one had done it. When the king told the judge his problem, the great judge said, "Nearby is a temple that contains a bell that has wonderful powers. When a man who has not stolen touches it, the bell remains silent. However, it rings when it is touched by a thief." The king was delighted. He explained the test to his assistants and sent them all to the temple.

The judge had the bell placed behind a curtain in a small room and covered its surface with ink. He then took all the suspects to the room and had them put their hands through the curtain to touch the bell. When they took their hands out, the judge and the king examined them. Everyone's hands were stained except for one man's. This man was arrested and questioned. However, he kept saying he was not a thief. Even when he was beaten and tortured, he did not confess. But the king was convinced he was guilty and had him sent to jail for many years.

Lesson

Definitions of a Straight Line

PURPOSE

Lesson 18 explores how one can use a particular point of view to fulfill a specific purpose. The students will address the issue by examining various mathematical definitions of a straight line.

Students will:

- Examine multiple definitions of a straight line.
- Determine how and in what circumstances one definition might be better than another.
- Discuss the difference between choosing something because it is correct and choosing something because it is appropriate for one's purposes.

INTRODUCTION

In this week's lesson, the students consider a situation in which we all agree on what an object is, but we differ on the best way to describe it. A somewhat similar case arose in Lesson 5, in which Winslow Homer's *Hound and Hunter* inspired a variety of different stories. In that lesson, although the students may have thought that one story was clearly the best, they still considered other points of view. In today's lesson, the students explore the process of choosing among differing but correct accounts and using

BENCHMARK

The students know and understand the expectations of them in the discussion process and they are better at following directions and need almost no supervision to accomplish their individual and small group assignments. The students are also staying quiet while others are talking.

Lesson 18: Definitions of a Straight Line

reasons other than correctness to do so. This lesson raises the issue that, depending on our purpose, one particular viewpoint may be more or less appropriate or useful than others.

LESSON SUMMARY

We will explore this type of situation by considering a simple geometric object that will be familiar to all your students—a straight line. From our very first drawings as children, we become familiar with straight lines and with how hard it is to draw them. All our students are experts at recognizing them and are very proficient at deciding that a particular line is not straight, either because it is curved or bent. They are probably also very skilled at deciding that one line is straighter than another. Yet in spite of this high informal level of expertise, the students will likely find it very difficult to describe a straight line—one of the most difficult objects to define. Different people can have different, yet equally geometrically correct, ideas about what characterizes a straight line. Some people might describe a straight line by its looks, whereas others might describe the fact that it is the shortest distance between two points. Still others might select the fact that you can draw only one straight line between two points, whereas every other line between two points has a symmetrical match. Each of these descriptions is correct. One description might be most useful for drawing a straight line, another for deciding whether a line is actually straight, another for teaching someone what a straight line is, and still another for deciding which of two non-straight lines is the straighter one.

In question 1 of the Individual Work, the students are asked to draw a straight line without using any straight edge. Then they will draw a straight line using some aid like the side of a book or pencil, a tight piece of string, or even a ruler. Ask them why it was hard to draw a straight line freehand. Then have them answer question 3 in the Individual Work. This exercise will give them some experience in deciding when one line is straighter than others. In the large group discussion on the definitions, you will, as you did in Lesson 13 ("The Eagle"), act more like you do in a regular class session. You should be more active in helping the students understand each of the definitions and that each definition does describe a straight line. Encourage the students to consider reasons why some definitions seem better or worse to them or seem harder or easier for them to understand. Some possible uses of each definition are as follows:

- Definition 1 gives an important characteristic of a straight line—that it is the shortest distance between two points. However, some people might claim that this definition helps one draw a straight line but doesn't explain what it means to be straight.

- Definition 2 shows how straight lines differ from other lines that would move when rotated. This analysis wouldn't help one draw a straight line but might be useful in determining whether a line is straight.

- Definition 3, looking down the straight line and seeing only a point, does not give a test or a method for drawing but might be the most useful definition for explaining what a straight line is like.

- Definition 4, which says that only one straight line can be drawn between two points, might be most useful in doing geometry.

Your students may have other uses. What is important is that they see that the same object can be described in different and useful ways. Like Lesson 13, this lesson employs discussion to explore content.

Possible Questions to Raise

- How could we decide which definition is the best?
- If all the definitions are correct, how would we decide which one to use?
- Why do we need more than one definition of a straight line?
- Can you think of another way to describe a straight line?
- Can you think of anything else that has more than one definition that is correct?
- Are any of these definitions better than the others for deciding whether a line is straight?

Lesson 18: Definitions of a Straight Line

LESSON PLAN 18

| Activity | Time |

1. ARRANGE CLASSROOM .... 3 min.
  - Ask your students to sit in a circle.

2. INDIVIDUAL WORK .... 8 min.
  - Pass out the worksheet, explain the instructions, and have the students complete the Individual Work.
  - Ask the students why it is difficult to draw a straight line.

3. SMALL GROUP WORK .... 10 min.
  - Divide the class into small groups of four or five students.
  - Ask the group members to agree on an answer to question 3 in the Individual Work. Tell the students they should have a reason for their choice.

4. GROUP REPORTS .... 5 min.
  - Reconvene the large group and have the small groups report.
  - Remind them to explain how they decided which line was the straightest.

5. TEXT .... 2 min.
  - Read the text aloud while the students read along silently.
  - Have the students look at the definitions and illustrations, and make sure they understand them. Explain any with which they have trouble. Make sure that they know that each definition is legitimate.

6. DISCUSSION .... 12 min.
  - Ask the students which definition is most useful for drawing a straight line.

Total: 40 minutes

Worksheet 18: Definitions of a Straight Line

INDIVIDUAL WORK

1. Draw a straight line *without* any help.

2. Draw a straight line using any help or aid (like a ruler or book) you have with you.

3. Which of the following lines is straighter between points A and B? Circle your choice.

a)

c)

b)

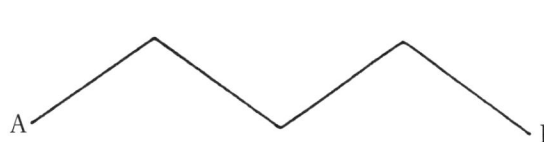

d)

TOUCHPEBBLES VOLUME A

147

SMALL GROUP WORK

1. Which line above does your group think is the straightest? If there are disagreements, discuss the differences until you can agree.
2. Why do you think that the line you chose is the straightest? You must have at least one reason for your choice.

Lesson 18: Definitions of a Straight Line

Definitions of a Straight Line
(STUDENT VOLUME, PAGE 43)

Ever since you were very young, you have probably been drawing pictures. Some of these drawings might have been of animals or trees, others might have been of buildings. Surprisingly, when we look at these pictures, we realize that the hardest thing to draw is a perfectly straight line. Because a straight line is the simplest line there is, this difficulty might puzzle us. In addition, although it is easy to tell when a line is not straight, it is very hard to tell whether a line is perfectly straight even when we draw it with a ruler.

Here are four ways of explaining to someone how to decide whether a line is perfectly straight. Think about which way is best or whether you can think of better ways.

1. A straight line is the shortest distance between two points.

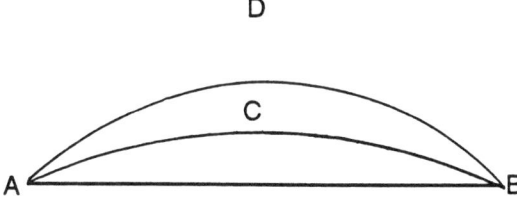

Line AB is shorter than line ACB and line ACB is shorter than ADB. If line AB is shortest of all lines between A and B, it is perfectly straight.

2. Imagine a straight line and a curved line drawn between two points, A and B, on a piece of paper. If you spin the paper around points A and B, the curved line moves but the straight line doesn't.

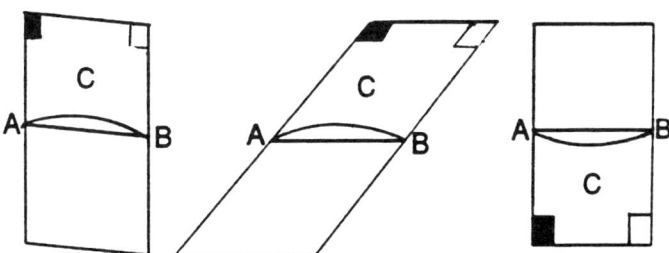

As the paper turns (follow marks ■ ☐), straight line AB doesn't move but curved line ACB does move.

TOUCHPEBBLES VOLUME A

Lesson 18: Definitions of a Straight Line

3. If you look down a straight line, you see only a point and no other part of that straight line.

   Looking along Straight line AB and all you see is a dot.

   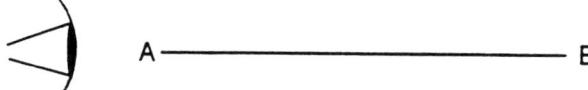

4. Between any two points, such as points A and B, you can draw only one straight line.

   There is only one possible straight line, AB.

Lesson

Gilgamesh the King
An Epic from Ancient Persia

PURPOSE

One of the convictions present in all Touchstones programs is that all people need one another in order to learn—about both the world and themselves. But to work well with one another, people must be able to give and receive critical comments.

Students will:
- Discuss a story in which a character is criticized.
- Examine how one's feelings for another person may determine whether one can receive criticism from him or her.
- Explore how and from whom they are able to receive personal criticism.

INTRODUCTION

What makes it possible for us to learn from other people? Must they be just like us in some important way? Or can we learn from a wide range of people: friends, teachers, parents, strangers, and even enemies?

Everyone has to learn important things about themselves. Sometimes we can learn these lessons on our own through the act of identifying with others and imagining how our behavior affects them. More often, however, we need the help of other people to get a clear perspective on ourselves, and determine whether we wish to change our behavior or our opinions or be confirmed in what we are doing. The fundamental question is, whose point of view are we willing to accept to learn something about ourselves?

Few of us like to admit that we need the kind of help that Gilgamesh so learly needs in "Gilgamesh the King." The Touchstones Method shows participants that even very talented people need the help of others. Everyone brings strengths and weaknesses to a discussion and everyone depends on the other members of the group to help them refine their strengths and overcome their weaknesses. For example, careful readers may need to learn to explore ideas with others; acute listeners may need to develop the ability to speak out; and articulate speakers may need to learn how to listen. Discussion is not meant to be a test of strength, but students may approach the discussion that way before settling down to discussion with people they have come to see as equals.

Lesson Summary

The ancient epic story of Gilgamesh explores the issue of accepting criticism from others. Gilgamesh is a very powerful king who has no compassion for his people. He works them so hard that they don't have enough time to tend to the welfare of their families. The story implies that Gilgamesh will listen only to someone he considers his equal. He finds such a person in the forest man. The forest man differs from Gilgamesh in upbringing and attitudes. For instance, he frees the animals caught in Gilgamesh's traps. But physically the forest man could be the king's twin. Gilgamesh's first impulse on seeing the forest man is to fight him. When he finds that he cannot defeat him, Gilgamesh offers his friendship; here at last is a man he can respect. However, the forest man replies that before they can be friends, Gilgamesh must become a just and caring king to his people. Gilgamesh laughs and agrees and does in fact become a great king.

In the story, although the people of Uruk see the forest man and Gilgamesh as equals, the king only accepts their equality after a test of strength. However, the forest man requires more than equality of strength. He will respect Gilgamesh only if the king changes his behavior and becomes caring and just. Some of your students will be like Gilgamesh, some like the forest man. The worksheet will assist them in determining what they require to respect and learn from another person. A goal of Touchpebbles is to create enough mutual respect so that students who normally do not associate with one another can tell one another important things and help one another learn. To achieve that, the students need to explore how and when they are likely to listen to others and whether it is possible to hear truths about themselves from those who are not their "second selves."

Possible Questions to Raise

- What does it mean when Gilgamesh calls the forest man his "second-self"?
- Would Gilgamesh react to the forest man's comments the same way if he did not think he was his equal?
- Why is the forest man able to talk to Gilgamesh the way he does?
- Have you ever become friends with someone you did not like at first? How did it happen?
- Why is it hard to take criticism from other people without getting mad?
- If you were Gilgamesh, would you have reacted the same way to the man's comments?

Lesson 19: Gilgamesh the King

LESSON PLAN 19

| Activity | Time |

1. ARRANGE CLASSROOM..3 min.
   - Ask the students to sit in a circle.
2. INDIVIDUAL WORK ....8 min.
   - Pass out the worksheet.
   - Read the questions aloud and answer any questions the sudents might have. Ask them to answer both questions, which should help them identify someone from whom they could accept criticism.
3. SMALL GROUP WORK ....8 min.
   - Divide the class into groups of four or five students and ask them to share their answers to questions 1 and 2 in the Individual Work with one another. After a few minutes, the students should try to agree on two responses to question 2.
4. GROUP REPORTS...5 min.
   - Reconvene the large group and have the small groups share the two items they agreed on. Make a list of all the items to see whether one item is on everyone's list.
   - Discuss the tally as the reports are given, but make sure every group reports.
5. TEXT ....2 min.
   - Read the story aloud the students read along silently.

6. DISCUSSION ....14 min.
   - To encourage the students to begin with evidence from the story itself, ask them why they think Gilgamesh listened to the forest man. Ask the students whether they could imagine some other character who could persuade the king not to be so cruel. Toward the end of the discussion, ask the students: What kinds of things about yourself can you learn best from strangers? From friends? From classmates?

Total: 40 minutes

TOUCHPEBBLES VOLUME A

Worksheet 19: Gilgamesh the King

INDIVIDUAL WORK

1. Suppose you were mean to one of your friends. For example, maybe you spread a story about him or her. Who could persuade you to apologize and make you feel good about it? Choose one from the list below:

    ❏ My parents
    ❏ My sister or brother
    ❏ My best friend
    ❏ The person I was mean to
    ❏ Someone I didn't know very well who saw it happen
    ❏ A friend of the person I was mean to
    ❏ Other_____

2. What is the best kind of person to persuade you that you have done something wrong and should apologize? Check all that apply.

    ❏ Someone who is my age
    ❏ Someone who is a boy like me or a girl like me
    ❏ Someone who is a good student
    ❏ Someone who is fair
    ❏ Someone who lives near me
    ❏ Someone who usually tells me good things about myself
    ❏ Someone who likes to play the same games
    ❏ Someone who is a relative (brother, sister, cousin, etc.)
    ❏ Someone who is the same size as I am
    ❏ Someone from the same kind of family

SMALL GROUP WORK

1. Compare your answers to question 1 in the Individual Work.
2. Compare your answers to question 2 in the Individual Work, and try to agree on two choices.

Lesson 19: Gilgamesh the King

Gilgamesh the King
An Epic from Ancient Persia
(STUDENT VOLUME, PAGE 45)

Gilgamesh was a very cruel ruler of the city called Uruk. He made his people work such long hours that they had very little time to gather food for themselves or take care of their families. The people of Uruk were very unhappy and prayed for help for many years. Finally, their prayers were answered. A man appeared who was as strong as Gilgamesh and who looked just like the evil king. He lived in the forest and soon became a good friend to all the animals. One day, one of the king's hunters saw this man undoing the animal traps that the king had set and the hunter ran back to tell Gilgamesh. The king became very angry and had soldiers bring this forest man into the city.

When the people saw the man of the forest, they thought he was Gilgamesh because he was so proud and handsome and strong. However, they were startled when their king came out of the palace. They looked at these two men who could have been twins and held their breath, not knowing what would happen.

Gilgamesh raced forward and hit the forest man in the face. However, the forest man jumped right back up from the ground and struck the king in the chest. The king had never been hit that hard before and fell down. The two men kept fighting but neither could defeat the other. Finally the king said, "Enough! Why are we fighting? We are equal in strength and we look like brothers. You are my second self. Come, let us be friends and stand together against the enemies of my people."

The forest man got up from the ground and offered his hand to help Gilgamesh. "If we are to be true friends, you must hear my words. I will stand with you against the enemies of your people, but right now you yourself are their greatest enemy. We can be friends only if you become a just and caring king. Otherwise we must keep on fighting, and, as you can see, neither of us can beat the other."

Gilgamesh was so amazed that he stood there with his mouth wide open. He looked as though he had been struck by lightning. He was such a mighty king that no one had ever spoken to him like that before. Even if someone had tried to give him advice, the king wouldn't have listened because no one was his equal. A smile crossed Gilgamesh's face and he began to laugh. He stretched out his hand to his equal and followed the words of his new friend.

Lesson 19: Gilgamesh the King

DISCUSSION EVALUATION SHEET 5

High levels of participation and a general sense of cooperation among all your students should be regular characteristics of your Touchpebbles Discussions at this point. This stage of your group's work history should be focused on developing active listening skills, critical thinking and critical reading skills, and high-level cooperation skills characterized by students' recognizing the importance of working as a group. These skills cover a broad spectrum, and your students will likely be at very different places along this continuum.

Because of the differences in students' progress, most of your questions during the discussion should help model the types of listening, thinking, and cooperation skills that will take the students to the next level of discussion. For example, For example, the students should work on building on what others have said. Through modeling and questioning, you can guide them to recognize the interconnectedness of their opinions and whether they agree or disagree with previous comments. Furthermore, as the students become more concerned with increasing their understanding of a topic or text, they will often need guidance to learn how to ask questions that will increase their understanding and help them learn from others.

Teaching students that they can learn from their peers is an important part of the Touchpebbles program. It can be accomplished by improving cooperation, listening, thinking, and speaking skills. The discussions will then be true cooperative inquiries, and the students will be both participants and leaders. This ideal may rarely be met, particularly among young students, but each area can be targeted and developed through your leadership.

Are the students stating their ideas clearly?
❑ Never ❑ Sometimes ❑ Often ❑ Always

Are the students following the lines of discussion and thought?
❑ Never ❑ Sometimes ❑ Often ❑ Always

Are the students accepting of other opinions?
❑ Never ❑ Sometimes ❑ Often ❑ Always

Are the students building on each other's comments and responding directly to one another?
❑ Never ❑ Sometimes ❑ Often ❑ Always

Are you doing less talking and question asking than earlier in the year?
❑ Yes ❑ No

Do the students listen respectfully to one another?
❑ Never ❑ Sometimes ❑ Often ❑ Always

Lesson 19: Gilgamesh the King

Are the students interrupting one another less with each discussion?
❏ Yes   ❏ No

Are the students asking questions to help them understand the text?
❏ Never   ❏ Sometimes   ❏ Often   ❏ Always

Lesson 20

The Weapons of King Chuko
by Lo Kuan Chung

PURPOSE

In previous lessons, the students have considered what to say and ways to say it. In this week's lesson, they will focus on another aspect of language: when, if ever, something should be said. They will address the issue by examining a familiar problem: bragging.

Students will:
- Decide whether they would tell people about certain accomplishments or keep them secret.
- Examine a story in which a great accomplishment is kept secret.
- Compare their experiences with bragging with the actions of the characters in the story.

INTRODUCTION

To participate successfully in discussions, people must explore what is appropriate to say and also how and when to say it. During this year, the students have investigated different aspects of language that are relevant to discussions. They have experimented with the relationship of form and content and examined the differences between objective opinions and facts. In addition, they have practiced giving and accepting criticism, asking questions, and explaining their ideas.

Another communication issue is bragging. Many people are tempted to boast of success. In some societies, it is not socially acceptable to boast. In the Unites States, we are ambivalent about boasting and its counterpart, modesty. Those who reach pinnacles of success in business, sports, or entertainment are held in high esteem and are expected to flaunt their status. However, "showing off" and "tooting your own horn" are still phrases of rebuke. Someone who wears success and wealth with grace rather than ostentation is admired by many people.

Lesson 20: The Weapons of King Chuko

Elementary school students are often very aware of the pitfalls of boasting and modesty. They neither want their successes overlooked nor do they want to be called a show-off. They must decide when, if ever, they should speak of their accomplishments. For example, a student who does especially well on a test might be rightly proud. But if that student boasts, his or her peers may become resentful. This situation can be difficult and delicate for successful students. In the same way, the students who are successful in sports may get acclaim from others up to a point, but they may lose credibility if they are overly boastful.

Lesson Summary

This lesson's Individual Work asks the students to consider the issue of boasting by choosing whether they would reveal certain facts about themselves that most people would consider admirable. The Small Group Work explores why the students might wish to reveal certain things but not others. Furthermore, the students will explore when they would feel comfortable expressing pride in themselves and when they would rather have someone else single them out for their achievements.

The text tells the story of King Chuko, who knows he is clever, thoughtful, and shrewd, but who also is not boastful or explicitly proud. On the contrary, he acts modestly and deliberatively even to the point of appearing careless. His city is threatened by a large army, and, through cleverness, King Chuko thwarts the attack. However, after the enemy is fooled by the king's trick, King Chuko refuses to be praised and stops his subjects from celebrating.

Possible Questions to Raise

- Do you think the king's subjects could have held back from celebrating forever?
- Do you admire the king's behavior?
- What would happen in the future if all the people celebrated?
- What would happen if the enemy general learned later that a trick had been played on him?
- Why is bragging bad?
- Is bragging always bad?
- Why might you prefer for someone else to tell others about your accomplishments?
- Is King Chuko right to keep his victory a secret?
- Would it be OK to celebrate if King Chuko had won a great battle and made the enemy armies run home?

Lesson 20: The Weapons of King Chuko

LESSON PLAN 20

Activity	Time
1. ARRANGE CLASSROOM	1 min.

- Ask the students to sit in a circle.

2. INDIVIDUAL WORK .... 8 min.
   - Pass out the worksheet.
   - Have the students answer the questions.
   - Make sure they understand the questions and what they are to do. If they can't choose "yes" or "no" easily, tell them to pick the most likely answer and go on.

3. SMALL GROUP WORK .... 10 min.
   - Divide the class into groups of four or five students.
   - Ask the students to share their answers.
   - Ask them why some things are appropriate to tell everyone about and some things aren't.

4. TEXT .... 2 min.
   - Reconvene the large group and read the story aloud while the students read along silently.

5. DISCUSSION .... 19 min.

Total: 40 minutes

Worksheet 20: The Weapons of King Chuko

INDIVIDUAL WORK

1. Read each statement below, then decide whether you would want to tell your friends and everyone else about it. Check the box next to your answer.

   a) You win a big trophy in sports.
   ❑ Yes, I'd tell   ❑ No, I'd keep it a secret

   b) You live in a fine, large house with servants.
   ❑ Yes, I'd tell   ❑ No, I'd keep it a secret

   c) You score the highest grades on a state test.
   ❑ Yes, I'd tell   ❑ No, I'd keep it a secret

   d) Your parent is very famous.
   ❑ Yes, I'd tell   ❑ No, I'd keep it a secret

   e) You just received $500 from your relative.
   ❑ Yes, I'd tell   ❑ No, I'd keep it a secret

   f) You are the strongest person in school.
   ❑ Yes, I'd tell   ❑ No, I'd keep it a secret

   g) You play a musical instrument so well that you win a prize.
   ❑ Yes, I'd tell   ❑ No, I'd keep it a secret

   h) You are named "most beautiful" or "most handsome" in a contest.
   ❑ Yes, I'd tell   ❑ No, I'd keep it a secret

   i) You save someone's life.
   ❑ Yes, I'd tell   ❑ No, I'd keep it a secret

2. Is there one item on this list that you would want people to find out about you, but only from someone else?

   Write the letter here _____.

SMALL GROUP WORK

1. In your groups, compare your answers to the questions in the Individual Work.
2. Is bragging always bad? Discuss it as a group, and decide your group's answer. You should have at least two reasons to support your group's answer.

Lesson 20: The Weapons of King Chuko

The Weapons of King Chuko
by Lo Kuan Chung
(STUDENT VOLUME, PAGE 47)

Chuko was a great king, famous in war and loved by his people. His enemy, the king of a neighboring country, sent two great armies to destroy him. When the news came that two armies were approaching the city, all King Chuko's people were upset and afraid because their king had very few soldiers there. But King Chuko was calm. He sent a soldier to get some things for him and went to wait on the highest wall of the city. Soon the soldier brought him what he asked for: a colorful robe and a musical instrument. "Now I have the weapons I need," he said. Everyone was puzzled and afraid. "Now, do everything I say," King Chuko told his few soldiers. "Take down all the flags, open the city gates very wide, let some people go outside to work, and keep out of sight." Everyone thought that fear had caused him to lose his mind, but they followed his orders.

Soon the enemy armies halted some distance from the city, and the general and his officers spied on the city from a nearby hill. They saw King Chuko on the high wall, beautifully dressed, playing the instrument and singing, and they saw the city gate open and people working peacefully. His officers were eager to attack. One said "Look, we will win a great victory. They don't expect us. We will destroy them." The general was silent and studied King Chuko and the city. Finally, after much thought he said, "Tell my armies to march north and to stay 20 miles away from the city." "What?" said a young prince. "We must attack now."

"You are here to learn about war and this is your first lesson," said the general. "King Chuko must think I'm a great fool. He thinks I will fall into his trap. A great army is hidden in the city waiting to attack us." "How can you tell?" asked the prince. The general replied, "See the workers outside the city? King Chuko would never risk his citizens' lives."

After the armies left, King Chuko stopped singing and playing and came down from the city wall. All his people were amazed at the success of his weapons. They all wanted to celebrate. But their king refused to let them. He said, "No, we must not celebrate. We must look sad. What if our enemy sends scouts to watch the city? If we celebrate, they'll learn it wasn't a trap but a trick. Next time they will destroy us. This is a victory we must always keep a secret."

Lesson 21

The Odyssey
by Homer

PURPOSE

In Lesson 21, your students will evaluate a common way that people often judge others—by imagining themselves in another person's position.

Students will:
- Judge one another's explanations for a person's actions.
- Explore how understanding another person's reasons and motives can help explain his or her actions.
- Recognize the complexities of judging another person.

INTRODUCTION

Understanding another person's actions is often difficult. If we could imagine doing the same thing in the same case, we are tempted to judge the action as reasonable. Judging our own actions is more difficult because our familiarity with our own situation makes it almost impossible to ask ourselves why we do certain things. However, when someone else's action puzzles us, we probe more deeply into why he or she acted that way. Furthermore, we ask ourselves, sometimes for the first time, how we would have acted differently. By exploring such differences, we can uncover the reasons for our own actions.

When we first hear about an action that puzzles us, we may think that the person had no good reason for his or her action, and thus we avoid trying to figure out why someone did something we don't understand. However, if we are forced to

> **BENCHMARK**
> Discussions show signs of cooperative learning. Students build on what others say, and discussions sound more like an exploration of ideas rather than a succession of comments. Students, when speaking, may also refer to previous discussions—displaying a sense of group history.

TOUCHPEBBLES VOLUME A

consider the situation more closely, we can often see the other person's perspective and the action frequently starts to seem less foolish or silly than we first thought.

Understanding a person's perspective, involves understanding the person's circumstances as well as ourselves. Suppose someone gave $10,000 to another person. If we thought the donor was unknown to the benefactor, such an action might seem puzzling. However, if we discovered that the recipient had long ago helped the donor's family, the gift would begin to make sense. But what if we could not discover any previous connection between the two people? To make sense of this action, we would have to further consider the goals and motives of the donor. Doing this would also force us to consider our own goals and purposes.

LESSON SUMMARY

The text will help the students explore another person's motives. Through much of the story, the Greek hero Odysseus seems foolish or silly. However, some incidents in the tale also show how clever he is. Odysseus' foolish acts include entering into a strange cave to see whether he can get a gift, calling out to the blinded Cyclops after he and his men have escaped, and then calling out to the Cyclops a second time even after they were almost hit by a boulder and killed. The clever actions are Odysseus telling the Cyclops that his name was No One and figuring out a way to escape from the cave. The students should discuss how the same person who did the clever things could have done the seemingly foolish things. The dichotomy makes it possible to suggest that maybe he was not as foolish as he first appeared. You should also encourage the students to share situations in which they once thought someone did something foolish and later reconsidered their opinion. What did they find out that made them change their minds?

POSSIBLE QUESTIONS TO RAISE

- How can someone who is so clever also be so silly?
- Would you have done something different from what Odysseus had done?
- Have you ever changed your mind about someone's actions after you had learned more about why they did what they did?
- Can you think of any reasons that might make sense of silly things?
- Have you ever been wrongly judged by others because of something you did?

Lesson 21: The Odyssey

LESSON PLAN 21

Activity	Time
1. ARRANGE CLASSROOM	1 min.
2. INDIVIDUAL WORK	5 min.

- Pass out the worksheet. Have the students complete the Individual Work.

3. SMALL GROUP WORK .... 7 min.
   - Divide the class into groups of four or five students and have them a) agree on one of the seven statements that they all believe is silly and b) work together on question 2 to make up a plausible reason for the man's seemingly silly action. For example, if the students think it is silly to save a chair, one possible reason they might give to change that perception might be that the chair is a very valuable antique or that it was made for the man by his father.

4. GROUP REPORTS .... 7 min.
   - Reconvene the large group. Have the small groups report their reasons.

5. TEXT .... 7 min.
   - Read the story aloud while students read along silently. Clarify any facts if necessary.

5. DISCUSSION .... 13 min.
   - Begin by having students help you make two lists, one of all the smart things that Odysseus did and another of all the silly things he did. Write them on the board.
   - Let the whole class thoroughly discuss each item on the list—some students may see an act as silly whereas others may see it as brave or smart.

Total: 40 minutes

TOUCHPEBBLES VOLUME A

Worksheet 21: The Odyssey

i **INDIVIDUAL WORK**

Imagine that a man runs into a burning house. Below are some of the reasons he might give for doing that. Check the box for each reason that seems silly to you.

- ❑ He is trying to save his mother.
- ❑ He is trying to save his dog.
- ❑ He is trying to save his tropical fish.
- ❑ He is trying to save a chair.
- ❑ He is trying to save a picture.
- ❑ He is trying to show how brave he is.
- ❑ He is trying to put out the fire.

S **SMALL GROUP WORK**

In your small group, choose one of the examples that you marked as silly and make up an explanation so that reason no longer seems silly.

The Odyssey
by Homer
(STUDENT VOLUME, PAGE 49)

Odysseus and his men were tired and nearly starving from their long journey across the sea. When they reached an island, they hunted, ate, and rested. The next day, after a long sleep, Odysseus saw another rocky island nearby. "I think that is where the cyclopes live. I have always wanted to see these giant creatures." At first his men tried to stop him, but after a while twelve of Odysseus' men agreed to go. They rowed to the island and climbed a high cliff to reach a cave.

The cave was bigger than ten houses. In the back of the cave, they found some sheep and a great deal of cheese and other food. They all ate their fill and wanted to leave. But Odysseus refused. "No, I want to meet the Cyclops, the owner of this cave. He may give a present to a stranger visiting him." Soon the ground shook, and a giant with only one eye in the center of his forehead stood at the entrance. He was bigger than they could have ever imagined. He easily rolled a huge stone across the mouth of the cave. Odysseus thought it would take one hundred men to move that stone.

The giant saw the men standing as far away as they could in great fear. "Who are you? Are you pirates?" asked the Cyclops. "No, we are soldiers traveling home from war," answered Odysseus. "We ask for kindness, the kindness all men give to strangers and travelers." "What do I care what others do?" aksed the Cyclops as he grabbed two men and killed them and ate them. Then the giant fell asleep. Odysseus stood his ground, filled with anger. "I could kill him now," he thought, "but then we could never move that rock. We would be trapped." The next morning the Cyclops awoke, killed two more men and ate them, and then started his day. He moved the great rock, counted all his sheep as they ran to the fields, and then put the rock back as he left. As he watched, Odysseus thought of a plan.

He found a large stick belonging to the giant. It was more than six feet long. He sharpened one end and hid the stick. When the Cyclops returned, the Cycolps killed two more men. Hiding his anger and disgust, Odysscus said, "You must be very thirsty now." Odysseus offered the giant a very strong wine that he had brought with him. The giant loved it and kept drinking. "Stranger, tell me your name so I can thank you," said the Cyclops. "My name is No One," said Odysseus. The Cyclops replied, "Well, No One, my present to you is that I will kill you last." He laughed, drank some more wine, and fell asleep.

Moving quickly, Odysseus and his men took the sharp stick and pushed it into the giant's one eye, blinding him. He screamed in horrible pain. Other cyclopes came running to his cave and yelled in, "What's wrong? Is someone hurting you?"

"No One is in here! No One is trying to kill me!" When they heard this they said, "If no one is hurting you, you must be sick. Get some rest," they said, leaving him alone. The giant screamed in pain all night. In the morning, the Cyclops moved the rock and let the sheep out. Once they were out, he said, "Now I'll find you and kill you all." But he heard Odysseus calling him from outside, for he had already escaped and was in his boat. He and his men had hung on to the wool of the sheep's bellies and gotten out.

They could have gotten away safely, but Odysseus yelled to the Cyclops, "You should have been kinder to your guests!" At the sound of his voice, the giant threw a large rock at the boat and almost crushed it. The men rowed hard and got even farther away. Odysseus stood up to call out again. His men tried to stop him, but he wouldn't listen. "Cyclops, if anyone asks who blinded you, say it was Odysseus, King of Ithaca."

The Cyclops went crazy with anger and prayed to his father, the ruler of the sea. "Father, hurt Odysseus for what he has done to me. Make him suffer on his trip home." The giant's father heard him. In punishment, all Odysseus' men were killed in storms and accidents, and he got home only after ten years of hardship and pain.

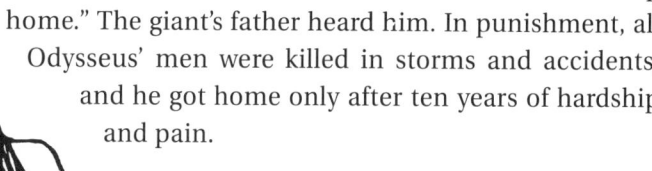

Lesson

How Much Is a Son Worth?
A Tale from Saudi Arabia

PURPOSE

In Lesson 22, your students will further explore the relationship between their public and private lives.

Students will:
- Recognize that people have both public lives and private lives.
- Consider a story in which a son's worth as a public figure (a future prince) is deemed to be greater than his worth as a private figure (a son).
- Determine whether their time in Touchpebbles Discussions has affected their lives outside the discussions—such as in other classes or at home.

INTRODUCTION

We all fill private and public roles. We are wives, husbands, sisters, or brothers at home, but teachers, principals, counselors, or colleagues at work. Adults experience this duality every day, but it will still be new to many of your students. The students at least know that their public roles as students require them to undertake responsibilities and duties unlike those they have at home. For example, as students, they follow regimented schedules, they study subjects they may not even like at the moment, and they must control their impulses by doing what others tell them to do rather than what they prefer to do. By contrast, in their private lives as children in families, they may enjoy much more freedom to do as they wish. It is very important for them to reflect on this public-private duality—which this week's text presents in a vivid way.

LESSON SUMMARY

Today's story tells of a prince who takes his son on a trip to learn about the world. While they are in a market area, the father lets his son go off to explore on

Lesson 22: How Much Is a Son Worth?

his own. However, the son is kidnapped and held for ransom. The prince wants his son back, but his response is puzzling. He offers less ransom every day. The students, like the kidnapper, probably would expect the opposite—that as each day went by the prince would be more anxious about his son and thus prepared to offer much more money for his safe return. However, as the prince explains to the kidnapper, each day the boy is held captive diminishes his ability to become a great ruler. How can the prince so easily distinguish between the boy as his son and as someone who will rule? Why is the boy's worth (as the title asks) based on his public role and not his private role as a son? After all, he will succeed his father as prince precisely because he is his son. The story seems to say that the prince cannot be like other fathers, and the son of a prince cannot be like other sons.

It may be very hard for students to view the father sympathetically. You might point out that their parents can love them as their children but still be very upset with them if they don't abide by their public duty to study hard and do well in school.

The tension between public and private personas has come up frequently this year in the context of the discussion classes. The Touchpebbles requires students to accept a more overtly public role as members of the discussion group. They must take responsibility for their own learning, for the overall success of the discussion, and for including everyone, even the students they might not like. Because the discussion lacks some of the formal features of a regular class—like raising hands—the students have to be more conscious of and more deliberate about, how they act toward others. The worksheet helps the students consider the skills that they are learning in Touchpebbles and helps them focus on some of the ways they need to improve during the rest of the year.

POSSIBLE QUESTIONS TO RAISE

- Why would the father pay less money each day to have his son back?
- Do you think a prince is worth more than an average person?
- Do you think the prince's son would be a better prince because of his captivity?
- Do you think the prince reduced the amount of money as a clever trick to get his son back?
- Do you agree with the prince's view of his son? Why or why not?
- Do think that being royalty should affect the relationship between the father and the son?

Lesson 22: How Much Is a Son Worth?

LESSON PLAN 22

Activity	Time
1. ARRANGE CLASSROOM	1 min.
2. INDIVIDUAL WORK	7 min.

- Pass out the worksheet.
- Have the students complete the section. This exercise encourages them to reflect on the Touchpebbles experience, so give them plenty of time.

3. SMALL GROUP WORK .... 8 min.

- Divide the class into groups of four or five students to discuss their answers to questions 1 and 2 in the Individual Work. The students may disagree, but ask them to make a list of one or two skills that everyone agrees they have learned since starting Touchpebbles and to consider whether they think any of these skills have carried over into their private roles outside school.

4. GROUP REPORTS .... 8 min.

- Have students return to the large circle so that each group can report on the items they listed. Make a list on the board. Ask whether the students can identify one or two skills that have been the hardest for them to learn.

5. TEXT .... 2 min.

- Read the story aloud while the students read along silently.

6. DISCUSSION .... 14 min.

- You might ask the students to imagine what skills someone would have to learn to be a good ruler and how he or she would have to change.

Total: 40 minutes

TOUCHPEBBLES VOLUME A

Worksheet 22: How Much Is a Son Worth?

INDIVIDUAL WORK

1. You have been in a Touchpebbles Discussion class for many weeks now. Pick one new skill you had to learn so that you could help make the discussions successful. Check any skills you have learned to do in class. If you've also begun to use that skill outside class, such as at home, underline the sentence.

   ❏ Listen carefully.

   ❏ Give reasons for what I think.

   ❏ Ask questions that might not have easy answers.

   ❏ Think about other people's ideas.

   ❏ Stop interrupting people when they are talking.

   ❏ Help other people get into the discussion.

   ❏ Not expect an adult to tell me all the answers.

2. Something I've learned that's not on this list is:

SMALL GROUP WORK

1. What have you learned in Touchpebbles Discussions? As a group, list two things that you have learned in your Touchpebbles class. They can be either skills (things you have learned how to do) or ideas that you came up with during discussions.

   a)

   b)

2. Do you use either of these things with your friends or in any other ways outside school? Explain how you do or do not use them outside school.

Lesson 22: How Much Is a Son Worth?

How Much Is a Son Worth?
A Tale from Saudi Arabia
(STUDENT VOLUME, PAGE 53)

A prince took his son on a trip to study the habits of many people so that he would be the best ruler possible. In each country, the prince and his son looked first at the libraries and other great buildings, and then the market area. In one country, there were many shops in the market and it was crowded with thousands of people. It was the perfect place to learn how people act toward one another. The father let his son go off alone to let him see everything and ask questions. The young prince was dressed in beautiful clothing and wore many rings. He was noticed by a poor man who had become a thief. The thief saw an opportunity and offered to guide the young man through the city. He led him to his own house instead and kept him there as a prisoner.

When a few hours passed and the young prince had not returned, the father became worried. He sent out his soldiers to different parts of the town offering a reward of 1000 pieces of gold for the return of his son. The kidnapper heard the offer, but thought he might get even more if he waited another day. The next day at around the same time, the desperate man again heard the soldiers in the street. However, this time the reward was only 500 pieces of gold. He thought he had not heard correctly and decided to wait yet another day. The next day the soldiers passed by once more. However, this time the reward was only 100 pieces of gold. Quickly the man took the boy back to his father.

When the boy was returned and the man had gotten his money, he asked the father why the reward had gotten smaller each day. "The first day my son was angry and refused all your offers of food, did he not?" asked the prince.

"Yes," said the man.

"On the second day, he took your offer of bread, and on the third day, he asked you for food, did he not?" asked the prince.

"Yes, that is just what happened," said the man.

The prince then explained, "Well, on the first day he was still a prince. He could still be a great ruler. However, on the second day he had become just like other people. If he became the ruler, he and his people would have to rule together. But by today, he begged for food just like any hungry person would. He was no longer worth anything to me as a ruler but only as my son. Were he ever to rule, he would be overthrown by others and would serve them."

TOUCHPEBBLES VOLUME A

Lesson 22: How Much Is a Son Worth?

Discussion Evaluation Sheet 6

As your class enters the final stages of your Touchpebbles Discussions, your focus should be on helping the students develop the critical thinking and reading skills that will make the most of their discussions. Their cooperation will remain a concern, but many of the recent lessons have asked them to assume various perspectives, solve problems, and reflect on their own opinions. The questions below can help you identify the ways in which your students are practicing these skills so that you can determine how best to lead them during the final lessons.

Are the students working with students with whom tthey might not otherwise?
❏ Never ❏ Sometimes ❏ Often ❏ Always

Are the students supporting their opinions with textual or experiential evidence and reasons?
❏ Never ❏ Sometimes ❏ Often ❏ Always

Are the students accepting of other opinions?
❏ Never ❏ Sometimes ❏ Often ❏ Always

Are the students building on one another's comments and responding directly to one another?
❏ Never ❏ Sometimes ❏ Often ❏ Always

Are the students identifying main ideas and questions about the topic?
❏ Never ❏ Sometimes ❏ Often ❏ Always

Are the students willing to explore various perspectives?
❏ Never ❏ Sometimes ❏ Often ❏ Always

Are the students working with students whom they otherwise might not?
❏ Never ❏ Sometimes ❏ Often ❏ Always

Do the students refer to past discussions or other classes?
❏ Never ❏ Sometimes ❏ Often ❏ Always

Are the students referring to and building on one another's ideas?
❏ Never ❏ Sometimes ❏ Often ❏ Always

Lesson 23

Images of Waves:
The Much Resounding Sea
by Thomas Moran
Waves at Matsushima
by Sotatsu

Purpose

In Lesson 13, your students discussed the advantages and disadvantages of three short texts about a common scene. Today's lesson will revisit this theme but will use two paintings as the point of comparison and contrast.

Students will:
- Evaluate the strengths of two paintings of the same subject.
- Consider how two paintings can express a common subject in different ways.
- Decide how they would present a subject to others.

Introduction

In Lesson 13 of this volume, the students explored three written versions of the same scene of an eagle that is perched on a cliff and then swoops down to the sea below. The three perspectives involved different ways of using language. None of the perspectives was right or wrong, but each had different advantages and disadvantages depending on the purpose and situation at hand.

TOUCHPEBBLES VOLUME A

Lesson 23: Images of Waves

Lesson Summary

This lesson has a similar function, except that it involves pictures. The common element is the use of waves—great, rolling, crashing waves—in both pictures. What is different are the two highly contrasting forms of presentation. The painting by Thomas Moran is realistic, not unlike a skillfully taken photograph. It shows us waves as we imagine we would see them if we visited the seashore on a blustery day. The one by Sotatsu, featuring gold and pigment on a large folding screen (the vertical lines in the photograph are the folds of the screen), depicts highly stylized waves with swirls and finger-like edges. No one has ever seen waves quite like these, yet they are unmistakably waves. For the discussion to be useful and meaningful, it should focus not on which painting is better but on supplying differing contexts so that the advantages of each perspective can become clear.

To prepare the students to discuss the paintings, the worksheet asks them to compare feature-length animated films and movies to decide which is appropriate under different conditions. For example, what are the pros and cons of using such animated films as *Shrek* or *Toy Story* as opposed to live-action movies to tell similar stories? In small groups, the students should first share their answers to the worksheet and then discuss and list what animated films and movies do best. They should report these lists in the large group discussion so that you can create a master list for the class.

Finally, in the large group discussion, have the students view and compare the two paintings. Have the students consider what one picture can do that the other can't and what each artist sacrifices to get the effects he wants. The class should consider whether the finger-like shapes at the tips of the waves on the Japanese screen are more or less like waves than are the spray and foam in the Moran painting. As the students explore the differences between the paintings, they might reconsider the differences between cartoons and movies. Movies with live actors share certain similarities with the Moran painting. Such movies are similar to what we might experience in real life but are created by a writer with a definite script. The Japanese painting, like the animated feature, is highly imaginative and even exaggerates certain features to help us notice elements that we might not ordinarily see, such as the tips of the waves.

Possible Questions to Raise

- How are both paintings good pictures of waves?
- Do the paintings reveal similar things about waves?
- Which waves would you least like to be in the middle of? Why?
- Do you think the artists' paintings have similarities? If so what are they?

Lesson 23: Images of Waves

LESSON PLAN 23

Activity	Time
1. ARRANGE CLASSROOM	1 min.
2. INDIVIDUAL WORK	7 min.

- Pass out the worksheet and have the students complete the section.
- Remind them to think of reasons for each answer.

3. SMALL GROUP WORK . . . . 10 min.
- Divide the class into groups of four or five students and ask them to compare their answers to the Individual Work.
- Ask the students to discuss and make a list of what animated films do best and what movies with live actors do best.
- *Note:* If you have the time, you could also display caricatures or drawings of famous people alongside photographs of the same people. Ask the students to list differences and ask whether photos are always better. What can caricatures do that photos can't?

4. GROUP REPORTS . . . . 7 min.
- Reconvene the large group. Have the small groups report on what kinds of things movies do best and when it's better to use a cartoon. Write the lists for each on the board.

5. PAINTINGS . . . . 2 min.
- Show the students the paintings. Explain that both pictures show waves.

6. DISCUSSION . . . . 13 min.

Total: 40 minutes

Images of Waves:
The Much Resounding Sea
by Thomas Moran
Waves at Matsushima
by Sotatsu
(STUDENT VOLUME, PAGE 77)

The paintings for this lesson are located on page 235

TOUCHPEBBLES VOLUME A

Worksheet 23: Images of Waves

INDIVIDUAL WORK

1. If you wanted to make a movie about the prince's kidnapped son (Lesson 22), would it be better to do it as—

    ❏ A movie with real people?   ❏ An animated cartoon?

2. If you wanted to make a movie about how bears live (how they fish, eat, sleep, play, grow up, and so forth), would it be better to do it as—

    ❏ A movie with real animals?   ❏ An animated cartoon?

3. If you wanted to make a movie about the story of the lion and the mouse (Lesson 5), would it be better to do it as—

    ❏ A movie with real animals?   ❏ An animated cartoon?

4. If you wanted to make a movie about your family so that people would know how you really live, would you do it as—

    ❏ A movie with real people?   ❏ An animated cartoon?

For each of these questions, be ready to give a good reason for your choice.

SMALL GROUP WORK

1. Compare your answers to the questions from the Individual Work.
2. Make a list of what animated cartoons (like a Disney movie) do best and a list of what movies with live actors do best.

Lesson

About Lying
by Michel de Montaigne

PURPOSE

Language is a central theme that is visited throughout the year in your Touchpebbles Discussions. In Lesson 24, your students will examine and discuss the occurrence of lying.

Students will:
- Discuss publicly a topic that is anything but public—lying.
- Compare their own experiences with lying to the author's ideas about lying.

INTRODUCTION

During this year, your students have experienced many dimensions of language with which they were previously unfamiliar. In the Touchpebbles lessons, they have probably begun to sense both the power of language and the problems it can cause.

In previous lessons, the students have seen in various ways that what was said, how it was said, and when it was said are equally important. In discussions, the students could see that communication would break down if a student couldn't state a thought clearly, used words that were unfamiliar to the other students, or used language improperly. Furthermore, the students' tone of voice, word choice, and manner of speaking could determine whether what the students said encouraged or discouraged discussion. Finally, the students could see the importance of

> **BENCHMARK**
> Listening skills and understanding among your students are improving. Students are now more frequently supplying reasons and evidence for their opinions and observations. They are referring to the text on their own, rather than being guided to the text by you.

Lesson 24: About Lying

timing and the effects of making remarks the class was not ready to hear or repeating ideas that the class was finished with.

Increasingly the students will recognize that words hold us together as human beings but can also keep us apart. Language makes it possible for us to experience the most precious emotions of friendship and love as well as the harshest feelings of anger and hatred. Language makes cooperation possible and brings complex societies into existence, but it can also tear societies into factions and create sustained conflict and war. Language is so deeply a part of what we are that it is perhaps impossible to imagine a human being without language.

Although humans may not be the only species with language (at some point, you may want to have students discuss whether they think animals possess language and how it works), humans are likely the only species capable of a very complex and all-too-common linguistic act: lying. A liar deliberately presents a set of words as true when the liar knows or believes those words are not true. Part of telling a lie, therefore, involves recognizing the difference between what is true and what is false. Although saying things that are true is the most important way we use language, a possibility always exists that language can be used to tell a lie.

Lesson Summary

The text by Michel de Montaigne will enable the students to discuss the issues that surround lying. Montaigne first contends that lying successfully is very difficult. If the lie is entirely made up, it's hard to remember. If, conversely, the lie is close to the truth, then frequently the liars get mixed up. Furthermore, if people discover that a person is good at lying, then that person will find lying more difficult. Montaigne also points out that a liar cannot take credit for telling lies. Montaigne believes that lying is one of the most serious dangers human beings confront. He claims that words hold us together and that lying threatens these bonds. He argues that children should be most seriously punished for lying because it is a habit that, once developed, is extremely difficult to break. These are issues that you should encourage your students to consider. Although Montaigne's text specifically deals with lying, such communication is just one of the ways in which language, while essential and valuable, brings great risks. For example, language can be used to encourage people but also to discourage them. Encourage the students to consider ways language can be a positive as well as a negative force.

Possible Questions to Raise

- Do you agree with Montaigne that humans are held together by words?
- Do you agree that lying is as bad as Montaigne says it is?
- Are there other reasons why lying is bad?
- Do you think it is hard to lie?
- Have you ever been caught lying?
- Do you think it is easier to lie or to tell the truth? Why?
- How would lying in a Touchstones Discussion be bad?

Lesson Plan 24

Activity	Time
1. Arrange Classroom	1 min.
2. Individual Work	7 min.

- Pass out the worksheet.
- Have the students complete the Individual Work.

3. Small Group Work .... 10 min.

- Divide the class into groups of four or five students and have them share their answers.
- The students will disagree over the gray areas.
- Ask the students to decide which is the most serious lie and why they think so, as well as which is most clearly not a lie and why they think so.

4. Group Reports .... 7 min.

- Bring the students back into the large circle, and ask the small groups to report on what they agreed was the worst lie and what wasn't a lie.
- Ask the groups to explain their reasons.
- Discussion may begin as the students try to assess the reasons. This is fine, but make sure each group gets a chance to report.

5. Text .... 2 min.

6. Discussion .... 13 min.

Total: 40 minutes

Worksheet 24: About Lying

INDIVIDUAL WORK

Check the sentences below that you think are lies.

❑ 1. Bob asks Joe how to get somewhere, and Joe tells him he thinks it's that way. Later Joe discovers it was another way.

❑ 2. Bill asks Mary whether she likes what he is wearing, and Mary says yes even though she doesn't.

❑ 3. A bully asks John where John's best friend is. John knows but says he doesn't know.

❑ 4. Mr. Smith catches Francis looking at Pat's test paper, but Francis denies it.

❑ 5. In a discussion, Sue repeats what other people have said instead of saying what she thinks.

❑ 6. Eric broke a school window with a rock, and David saw him do it but doesn't say anything to anyone.

❑ 7. Tom broke a friend's favorite toy but says he didn't do it.

❑ 8. Cathy is having trouble in school. Mrs. Jones, the teacher, tells her that she will succeed if she studies hard.

SMALL GROUP WORK

1. Share your answers from the Individual Work and agree as a group on which example was the most serious lie. Explain why your group made that choice.

2. Agree on which example most clearly was not a lie. Explain why your group made that choice.

About Lying
by Michel de Montaigne
(STUDENT VOLUME, PAGE 57)

People who lie either completely invent what they say or they change and hide something that is true. In either instance, it is very easy to trap them if you ask them many questions. When they lie by changing something that is true, they keep getting mixed up by the truth. What they know is true is more firmly in their minds than the lie that is so similar to it. The truth therefore keeps getting in the way. In situations in which they make up the whole story, it is hard for them to remember what they said. This is because there is nothing else in their minds that is similar to the lie.

Sometimes people are admired because they are good at lying. These people use words to please others and say what they think people wish to hear. But since people are so different, they must lie in different ways to different people. They tell one person that something is gray and another that it is yellow. But what happens if these people talk to each other about what the liar said? Also, it is hard to lie because if people know that you do it, they won't believe you. So if you're admired for your ability to lie, you will no longer be able to do it, since everyone knows you lie.

Lying is a very bad thing. We humans are held together only by our words. If we realized how bad lying is, we would punish it more than almost any other crime. It is silly that people often punish harmless faults in children. Only lying should get the worst punishment. Unlike most other faults, it grows with the child. Once children have started to lie, it is very difficult to change them.

Lesson 25

The Man Who Thought He Could Do Anything
A Tale of the Algonquin People

PURPOSE

In the previous lesson, your students dealt with the destructive nature of lying and how it can affect how others perceive you not only in your everyday life but also in Touchpebbles Discussions. Today's lesson will focus on building cooperation among your students.

Students will:
- Examine the benefits of working together as a group.
- Explore their own willingness to cooperate and work with others.

INTRODUCTION

Students are often tempted to make learning something they do on their own. Schools often reinforce this perception in assigning grades, since many students consider grades a mark of individual effort and accomplishment. Thus it becomes especially easy for bright students to believe that they must learn only by themselves. Students who don't do well in school may also believe they should not seek help. However, these students need to see that it is not possible to do everything themselves. This understanding will be especially true when your students eventually enter the workforce. Contrast the need for teamwork today with the early years of the industrial revolution in which a high degree of individual specialization was thought to be the best approach to manufacturing and even to intellectual research and scholarship. Although such an approach involved an extremely complex interdependence among workers, each worker had a solitary and very precise task to master. Work therefore did not require real skills of cooperation. The factory assembly line is the model of this approach.

Over the last thirty years, as computers and technology have advanced, this previous model has become nearly obsolete. People now need to learn how to cooperate with others who have very different skills and backgrounds. Solving any real problem or task requires input from a variety of people from different professions. Many of your students probably had doubts about a process like Touchpebbles that encourages collaboration. Discussion—like other types of learning—is something that no one can do alone. In the traditional school setting, students focus on mastering specific skills, often using and practicing them on their own. In Touchpebbles, respecting and cooperating with others are skills that are practiced and developed. These additional skills will help students adequately use the specific skills they learn in content classes. If students believe they must do everything alone, they will accomplish very little.

Lesson Summary

This week's story describes a person who feels a great need to do everything alone. Manabozho is a powerful wizard who is consumed by pride. His pride comes from his confident belief that he can do anything. In the story, he tries to do what he sees a baby do (an attempt that will probably strike your students as silly). Because his body is no longer as flexible as the baby's body is, however, he fails. The desire to do everything leads to absurdities and an inability to distinguish between what one must do alone and what one must do with the help of others, and between what is worth doing and what is a waste of time. Going it alone can also lead to despair, as in, how am I ever going to learn this? Manabozho feels this despair. He has set such a strange and high standard for himself that failure even in this one small activity causes him to doubt his other abilities. It also makes him lash out at others as if they were at fault. He shows his anger by turning an innocent boy into a tree.

The students must explore for themselves when it is appropriate to do something alone and when it is better to seek help. Every learner knows that there is too much to learn and certainly far too much to learn by themselves. The discussion may also raise the question of the role of the teacher. Should the teacher be expected to know all the answers? What is the purpose of education in general?

As a teacher, you are probably aware of the benefits of cooperative learning. Now your students will have an opportunity to understand cooperation a little better, even as the discussion method requires and trains them to be able to do it. The worksheet will help the students think about cooperation issues by focusing them on what they think is better to learn alone and what is better to learn with the help of others. The Lesson Plan suggests that you ask the students what difference it would make to the discussion class if the teacher were to grade everyone.

Lesson 25: The Man Who Thought He Could Do Anything

POSSIBLE QUESTIONS TO RAISE

- Why do you think Manabozho felt he had to do just what the baby did?
- Why do you think that turning the boy into a tree made Manabozho feel better?
- Would you like Manabozho in your Touchpebbles Discussion class? Why or why not?
- Is it easier to do your homework by yourself or with others?
- Are there things that are difficult about working with others?
- Do you have to cooperate with one another in a Touchpebbles Discussion?
- How does working in a group help you?

Lesson 25: The Man Who Thought He Could Do Anything

LESSON PLAN 25

| Activity | Time |

Activity   **Time**

1. ARRANGE CLASSROOM . . . . 1 min.
2. INDIVIDUAL WORK . . . . 7 min.
   - Pass out the worksheet.
   - Have the students complete the Individual Work.
3. SMALL GROUP WORK . . . . 10 min.
   - Divide the class into groups of four or five students and have them share their answers to the Individual Work. If there is disagreement, let the students provide and explore reasons why the item is best learned alone or with assistance.
4. DISCUSSION PART 1 . . . . 2 min.
   - Ask the students to form the large circle again. Tell them that the Touchpebbles Discussions are not graded, but ask: If a teacher wanted to grade the students, how could it be done? What effect would grades have on the Touchpebbles Discussions?
5. TEXT . . . . 2 min.

6. DISCUSSION PART 2 . . . . 18 min.

Total: 40 minutes

Worksheet 25: The Man Who Thought He Could Do Anything

INDIVIDUAL WORK

Check the box that describes the best way for you to do the following activities.

	By myself	With help from others
a) Learning to play tennis	❑	❑
b) Learning to run long distances	❑	❑
c) Learning to draw pictures	❑	❑
d) Learning to cook	❑	❑
e) Learning to fish	❑	❑
f) Learning to ride a bike	❑	❑
g) Learning arithmetic	❑	❑
h) Learning to shoot a basketball	❑	❑
i) Memorizing a list of important dates	❑	❑
j) Practicing an instrument	❑	❑
k) Learning to write neatly	❑	❑

SMALL GROUP WORK

Share your answers with one another. If you disagree with another student on an answer, explain the reasons for your choice.

Lesson 25: The Man Who Thought He Could Do Anything

The Man Who Thought He Could Do Anything
A Tale of the Algonquin People
(STUDENT VOLUME, PAGE 59)

Manabozho was a great and powerful wizard. He went from tribe to tribe doing many great deeds and was looked up to by everyone. He became so powerful that he began to think he could do anything. His deeds were wonderful, and every day he grew more and more proud of himself. He expected everyone to treat him with great respect, and he looked down on those who were not as strong or smart as he was. One day while walking through the forest feeling good about himself, he came to a campsite. There he saw a young child lying in the sunshine. The child was curled up resting and had his toe in his mouth.

The wizard Manabozho was amazed. He looked with great wonder at how the child was lying on the ground. "I've never seen a child do that before. But if a child can do it, I'm sure I can do it too." So he lay down beside the child to imitate him and curled his body just like child's. He took his right foot in his hand and moved it toward his mouth. But no matter how hard he tried, his foot stayed far from his lips. He tried again with his left foot but found that he failed again. He twisted his body every way he could think of, bent his arms and legs, and stretched his neck, but he couldn't do what the child did. As he was doing this, the little child opened his eyes, released his toe, stretched out, turned over, and in a moment had the toe of his other foot in his mouth. The warm sun made the baby make cooing sounds as he fell back asleep.

The wizard watched the baby and was very angry. "I cannot do it," he said, rising. "Perhaps all my great power is gone." He heard the cooing sounds and thought the baby was laughing at him. Angry and sad, he thought about taking revenge, but his attention was caught by some noise in the forest. He walked quickly into the forest and saw a young boy on a path. The boy was not paying any attention and ran into the wizard. Very angry, the wizard said, "Have you no respect for me?" "It was an accident," said the boy. Unhappy and in a rage, the wizard said, "You will never run again," and at that moment the boy was turned into a tree. "At least I can still do something," said the wizard, starting to feel good about himself again.

Lesson 26

Robinson Crusoe
by Daniel Defoe

PURPOSE

In Lesson 26, your students will discuss how the choices people make have both positive and negative consequences and how final decisions usually don't involve clear right or wrong choices.

Students will:

- Examine a number of circumstances and assess the positive and negative aspects of each.
- As a group, think of and analyze choices that have either good or bad consequences—not both.
- Attempt to explain why the main character of the text reacted the way he did.

INTRODUCTION

Most of the dual perspectives that we have considered so far this year involved trying to view something as it would be seen by someone else. This lesson is different. The students are asked to consider a single situation and draw two sets of consequences, one set that they consider good, the other bad. Most of the decisions they will make in life and work involve both positive and negative ramifications. What we eventually decide to do involves a sort of calculation about what is better or worse rather than what is simply good or bad. This lesson gives the students practice in evaluating evidence and consequences as well as in decision-making.

Lesson 26: Robinson Crusoe

LESSON SUMMARY

The text for Lesson 26 is from an early part of the story of Robinson Crusoe's life on an island. Crusoe's ship sinks and he washes up on shore alone. After taking care of his immediate needs for a hut, some food, and fire, he makes two lists; on one side he lists the bad aspects of his life, on the other side, the good parts of the same aspects. The text for the students includes two complete elements from Robinson Crusoe's long list: having no clothes and being alone. Having no clothes can be seen as bad because it is embarrassing and uncomfortable, or it can be seen as good because the weather is always warm, so he doesn't need clothes, and he is alone, so there is no chance of embarrassment. Second, being alone can be bad if one emphasizes the lack of friendship, but it can be good if one realizes that at least one doesn't have anyone with whom to argue and disagree. The third item in the list, on the "Bad" column, is not having friends.

The worksheet asks the students to continue the list on their own, adding a "good" item for two "bad" items that are given. In small groups, the students try to find both a "good" and a "bad" event or thing for which they cannot think of a corresponding "good" or "bad." The students must decide whether something can be entirely good or entirely bad.

POSSIBLE QUESTIONS TO RAISE

- If you thought you were alone on an island, would you be excited and glad if you found a fresh footprint in the sand or would you become worried and frightened like Robinson Crusoe was?
- Do you think it is easier to see the good in something or the bad? Why?
- What is another thing that you think would be "good" in Robinson Crusoe's life?
- What would be the hardest thing to get used to if you lived on an island alone?
- Have you ever had to make a choice or decision but believed that it was equally good and bad?

LESSON PLAN 26

Activity   Time

1. **ARRANGE CLASSROOM** .... 1 min.
2. **TEXT** .... 2 min.
   - Read the story aloud while the students read along silently.
   - Point out the list, and explain that Robinson Crusoe is looking at the same aspect of his life from two points of view.
3. **INDIVIDUAL WORK** .... 7 min.
   - Pass out the worksheet and have the students complete the section.
4. **SMALL GROUP WORK** .... 7 min.
   - Divide the students into groups of four or five students.
   - Have the group members share with one another what they added to Crusoe's "good" list.
   - Have them answer question 2 in the Small Group Work.
5. **GROUP REPORTS** .... 8 min.
   - Have the students come back to the circle to report their always "good" and always "bad" things.
   - Ask the class to think of ways that these "good" or "bad" things might be seen in the opposite light.
   - List the hard ones on the board and consider them later, but don't force the students to find a negative or positive viewpoint if they don't want to.
6. **DISCUSSION** .... 15 min.
   - Discuss Crusoe's finding of the footprint and how the students would feel in his place.

Total: 40 minutes

Lesson 26: Robinson Crusoe

Robinson Crusoe
by Daniel Defoe
(STUDENT VOLUME, PAGE 61)

On September 30th, 1659, I, poor, unhappy Robinson Crusoe, was shipwrecked during a dreadful storm and came to shore on this bare island, which I named the "Island of Despair." All others on my ship were drowned, and I was washed up almost dead. Over the next few days, several useful things were washed ashore from the destroyed ship, such as some tools, planks of wood, corn seeds, salted meat, and even a large chest of money. I smiled to myself as I thought how useless all that money was to me now.

With great difficulty and pain, I made myself a hut, planted the corn, and generally began doing daily jobs to help me survive. I continued this hard life for a year, at the end of which I made two lists. On one side, I wrote all the things which in this life alone on the island I called Bad; on the other side, I listed the Good.

Here is the beginning of my list:

Bad	Good
I have no clothes to cover me, but …	this island is in a warm part of the world, so I don't need any.
I am alone and have no one to speak to, but …	at least no one ever argues or disagrees with me.
I have no friends here, but …	

After many, many months, I was walking one day toward the little boat I had built when I was very surprised and shocked to see the print of a man's naked foot in the sand by the shore. I stood still like a statue, as if I had seen a ghost. I listened and looked around me, but I could neither hear nor see anything. I walked the beach but found no more footprints. I even went up in the hills but saw no one who could have made that footprint.

My heart beat faster as I went back to my hut, looking behind me at every two or three steps, looking behind bushes and up trees. I soon began to run to my castle (for so I pretended it to be now) and stayed there, too frightened to leave it. That night I did not sleep at all. In fact, the longer the time since I first saw the footprint, the more afraid I became. I kept thinking I saw a person when there was no one.

Worksheet 26: Robinson Crusoe

INDIVIDUAL WORK

Robinson Crusoe begins a list of bad and good ways of looking at parts of his life alone on the island. He has completed the first two. Complete the next two apparently bad things by finding a way to see them as good things.

Bad	Good
I have no clothes to cover me, but...	this island is in a warm part of the world, so I don't need any.
I am alone and have no one to speak to, but...	at least no one ever argues or disagrees with me.
I have no friends here, but...	_____
Many things that I like to eat I can't find or buy here, but...	_____

SMALL GROUP WORK

1. Share your answers from the Individual Work with your group members.
2. Write one thing that you all think is always good and cannot be seen is bad. Also think of one thing that seems always bad.

Only Good:

Only Bad:

Lesson 26: Robinson Crusoe

DISCUSSION EVALUATION SHEET 7

    With only four lessons left, your students should be taking more responsibility for the success of the discussions and exercising all the skills and behaviors that they have been developing throughout the year. They should be willing to explore the authors' and their classmates' opinions and ideas before judging them. They should be referring to past discussions, others' opinions, other classes, and their own experience. They should be paying attention to the speaker and building on what others say.

    Many of these skills are hard to measure. As you answer the questions below, think if different indications that the students might be progressing toward these skills. For instance, one question asks whether the students are seeking to understand one another's opinions. Asking a classmate a follow-up question or trying to restate a classmate's opinion are signs that a student is trying to learn from others. The questions may be easier to answer if you think of ways in which the students have changed during the year. If any other questions seem difficult to answer, think of individual students or different ways in which a skill or problem may appear; you will be able to better guage you students' skill levels.

Do the students refer to past discussions or other classes?
❏ Never ❏ Sometimes ❏ Often ❏ Always

Do the students ask questions to increase their understanding?
❏ Never ❏ Sometimes ❏ Often ❏ Always

Do the students ask questions to promote discussion?
❏ Never ❏ Sometimes ❏ Often ❏ Always

Have the students admitted changing their mind?
❏ Yes ❏ No

Are the students seeking to understand one another's opinions (as opposed to automatically agreeing or disagreeing)?
❏ Never ❏ Sometimes ❏ Often ❏ Always

Do the students support their opinions with textual references?
❏ Never ❏ Sometimes ❏ Often ❏ Always

Lesson 27

Narcissus
A Story from Greece

PURPOSE

Throughout the year, your students have been asked to listen to one another to have successful discussions. In Lesson 27, your students will help one another become better listeners and will learn why listening is such an important activity not only in discussions but also in all aspects of their lives.

Students will:
- Differentiate between listening to another person and hearing what one wants to hear.
- Identify situations in which someone is not listening to others.
- Examine their ability to listen to others.

INTRODUCTION

The entire year has been devoted to creating complex skills that will enable your students to improve their learning. Undoubtedly they have developed discussion skills individually and as a group. But other skills that emerge in a discussion environment are equally important. These skills will transfer to regular classes and enable students to gain more from your teaching. Central among these skills is the ability to listen. Listening is an active skill,

> **BENCHMARK**
> During discussions, the students are encouraging one another to speak. They assist one another in explaining ideas and ask helpful questions to clarify thoughts. Students are able to anticipate the next speaker and are aware of group dynamics such as silence and dominance.

Lesson 27: Narcissus

although we often think of it as passive. Many people have difficulty listening, but not because they have not heard the words that were uttered. Instead, they find listening difficult because people generally hear what they want to hear or already believe rather than what another person is really saying.

The tendency to hear only what we want to hear becomes a crucial problem in learning because often what we need to learn either conflicts or only distantly connects with what we already know and feel confident about. For instance, when people believed the sun went around the Earth, they often refused to listen to arguments that the Earth went around the sun. Similarly, in classroom learning situations, students who are good at language arts may be reluctant to approach new and different ideas in mathematics. Teachers face the ongoing challenge of building on what their students are comfortable with and can already do. Students with active listening skills and the ability to cooperate in their learning are more likely to meet other educational goals that their teachers have set for them. Without the ability to listen actively, students are unlikely to be able to undertake serious intellectual growth or be able to meet the demands of a technologically changing world. Without such listening abilities, the students would not be able to look beyond themselves—the downfall of the character in this lesson's story, "Narcissus."

Lesson Summary

This week's text presents the myth of Narcissus—someone who fell in love with his own reflection. Narcissus was very good looking and many people fell in love with him. However, he preferred his own company and kept himself apart from others. One day, tired from hunting, he stopped for a drink of water from a clear lake. When he leaned over the edge, he saw a very attractive face looking back at him. According to the myth, Narcissus fell in love with this face staring back at him from the water, never realizing that this face was his own. Captivated by his own reflection, he never moved and eventually wasted away.

In considering this story, the students must recognize that everyone must confront the challenge of recognizing that the "face" we love or the words we hear can often just be reflections of ourselves. You might start the discussion by asking the students how Narcissus could have figured out that the face was his own and continue by asking for the students' opinions on what Narcissus would have done if he had identified his reflection: would he have remained there or gotten up and left?

In this lesson, the students should consider the text first. After about ten minutes of discussion, have them complete the worksheet, which asks them to compare others to Narcissus and decide which case is most similar. After the students complete the worksheet, have them consider the distinction between hearing and listening. Learning how to listen takes years to master; participation in Touchpebbles Discussions provides students early on with concrete practice.

Lesson 27: Narcissus

POSSIBLE QUESTIONS TO RAISE

- What do you think good listening requires?
- Why do you think it upsets people when others do not listen to them?
- How could Narcissus have figured out that he was looking at his own face?
- Have you felt others were not listening to what you were saying even when they said they were? If so, how did you know they were not listening?
- What do you think you can do to learn to listen better?
- Why do you think it is important to listen to others?

Lesson 27: Narcissus

LESSON PLAN 27

| Activity | Time |

1. ARRANGE CLASSROOM . . . . 1 min.
2. TEXT . . . . 2 min.
    - Read the story aloud while the students read along silently.
3. DISCUSSION, PART 1 . . . . 10 min.
    - Begin the discussion by clearing up any details the students don't understand.
    - Ask them how Narcissus could have figured out that he was really looking at his own face.
4. INDIVIDUAL WORK . . . . 7 min.
    - Pass out the worksheet and ask the students to complete the Individual Work.
    - Make sure they understand that they are to circle the name of the person who is most like Narcissus and that they should think of a good reason for their choice.
5. SMALL GROUP WORK . . . . 8 min.
    - Divide the class into groups of four or five students and have them share their answers from the Individual Work.
    - See if it is possible for them to agree on which person is most similar to Narcissus.
6. DISCUSSION, PART 2 . . . . 12 min.
    - Have the students return to the large circle and ask the small groups to report.
    - Next, explore with the class the differences between hearing and listening.

Total: 40 minutes

Narcissus
A Story from Greece
(STUDENT VOLUME, PAGE 63)

Even as a little boy, Narcissus was very good looking. As he grew older, he grew even more handsome. By the time he was sixteen, he was so handsome that people fell in love with him just by looking at him. But he didn't want anything to do with anyone else; he just wanted to be by himself.

Once he was hunting in the forest when a lovely girl, whose name was Echo, saw him and fell in love at first sight. For a while, she only followed him around, but soon she came up to throw her arms around him and hold him. But Narcissus ran away from her and cried out, "Take your hands off me. Don't touch me. I'd rather die than have your hands on me." Echo was so sad and unhappy that she called after him, "One day I hope you fall in love with someone like I have fallen in love with you. You'll feel how awful it is when someone doesn't love you back."

One day soon after that, Narcissus became tired after hunting in the forest and came upon a beautiful lake surrounded by flowers and trees. No one had ever been in that part of the forest before. Narcissus was hot and thirsty, so he laid himself down by the lake and leaned over the edge to take a drink of water. At once he saw a face in the water, which was just like a mirror.

As soon as he saw the face, he stopped still, staring at it. He saw how good looking it was and soon fell deeply in love. He was so much in love that he couldn't take his eyes off the face in the water. All he knew was that if he moved at all, then the face also moved. It never occurred to him that he was in love with his own face. So he continued to lie very still, loving the face, until he wasted away because he would neither eat nor drink. Thus he died.

Worksheet 27: Narcissus

i **INDIVIDUAL WORK**

1. Some of the following people might be just like Narcissus—in love with themselves without even knowing it. Check the one who is most like Narcissus.

    ❏ a) John only likes people who think the same way he does.

    ❏ b) Mary only plays with people who dress and look like she does.

    ❏ c) When James listens to you, he only really pays attention to what he agrees with.

    ❏ d) Jack is always very worried about whether people like him.

    ❏ e) Susan only wants her friends to say nice things to her.

2. Why do you think the person you picked is most like Narcissus? Write down your reason.

s **SMALL GROUP WORK**

As a group, agree on which person from the Individual Work is the most like Narcissus.

Lesson 28

The Spider and the Turtle
A Tale of the Ashanti People of Africa

Purpose

In this lesson, your students will be exploring customs and, more implicitly, rules and how both customs and rules dictate what we say to, and do with, others.

Students will:
- Recognize the validity of other individuals' customs.
- Think of ways to make others feel welcome.
- Understand how customs and rules can make others feel excluded.

Introduction

We are used to thinking of customs as applying to the way people live in foreign countries, but each home has its own customs and is, in that sense, foreign territory, at least to others. Thus when we visit other people's homes, we learn to be prepared to abide by the rules of their house because we expect that our hosts will do some things differently than we do. Your students will have had experience with different home customs when they have stayed overnight at friends' homes. Customs of the house sometimes require only minor adjustments, like politely eating foods we are not used to. But customs may require visitors to make major changes. For example, students who pray before meals at home may visit friends who say different prayers or who do not pray at all. In this lesson, the students will begin to explore how differently people can live their lives and therefore how differently people can see the world. Different ways of seeing the world will concern us over the next three lessons. In Lesson 28, "The Spider and the Turtle," the students will consider the customs of their families and also the "customs" of the discussion class itself.

Lesson 28: The Spider and the Turtle

LESSON SUMMARY

The lesson begins with the students thinking of, and discussing in small groups, their favorite holidays and holiday rituals. Then the students explore the text, which tells how a spider avoided sharing his dinner with a turtle and how the turtle eventually got even. The turtle is lost in the forest and very hungry when he smells the delicious aroma of the spider's dinner. Spider law requires the spider to feed the turtle as a guest, but he doesn't really wish to abide by the spirit of that law. So he uses a custom, hand washing, to make it clear that the turtle is not welcome and to ensure that he won't have to share his food. The turtle treats the spider the same way when he visits later, so that the spider feels the same way the turtle did. It is an open question in the story whether the spider's the custom of washing hands or the turtle's custom of removing jackets removing are real customs or whether they are made up to prevent real hospitality without seeming overly greedy or revengeful.

Students may first notice and wish to discuss the clever trickery that goes on in the story. You should point out that the trickery is based on custom. Both the spider and the turtle use their customs to make the other feel unwelcome and to accentuate and even exaggerate the differences between them. Have the students discuss how hosts and guests should behave and how much, if at all, they should adapt to each other's customs. How do students behave differently when they are guests or hosts? Students may use the story to reflect on times when hosts have used customs to make them feel either welcome or unwelcome. Finally, broaden the discussion to focus on how customs are necessary for successful Touchpebbles Discussions. For example, every member of the group must follow the ground rules that make the discussion possible. You might also ask the students how well they think they are doing at following the customs, or ground rules, of the Touchpebbles class and whether the customs ever prevent people from playing a part in the discussion.

POSSIBLE QUESTIONS TO RAISE

- How could the spider have made the turtle feel welcome?
- Do either the turtle's or the spider's customs seem like a good customs?
- How could the turtle and spider make each other welcome in each other's homes in the future, despite what has happened?
- Have you ever felt unwelcome or out of place because of another person's rules or customs?
- Do you think the spider really wanted to help the turtle in the first place?
- Do you think the Touchpebbles ground rules are good rules?
- How would you make a new student feel welcome in your Touchpebbles class?

Lesson 28: The Spider and the Turtle

LESSON PLAN 28

Activity	Time
1. ARRANGE CLASSROOM	1 min.
2. INDIVIDUAL WORK, PART 1	5 min.

- Pass out the worksheet.
- Have students think of or jot down some answers to question 1. Do not deal with question 2 yet.
- *Note:* The purpose at this stage is to help define what a custom is and provide material for the students to share with one another. It may be a revelation to some children, for example, to hear how differently other children celebrate important holidays because they generally assume that all families are like their own.

3. SMALL GROUP WORK . . . . 10 min.
- Divide the class to into groups of four or five students and have them discuss their answers to question 1 in the Individual Work.

4. TEXT . . . . 2 min.
- Ask the students to come back to the large group.
- Read the story aloud while the students read along silently.

5. DISCUSSION, PART 1 . . . . 8 min.

5. INDIVIDUAL WORK, PART 2 . . . . 5 min.
- Ask the students to complete question 2.

5. DISCUSSION, PART 2 . . . . 9 min.
- Have volunteers share any additional Touchpebbles customs from question 2 in the Individual Work.
- Write the customs on the board and discuss whether these are in fact the customs of this group. There are general customs for the Touchpebbles class (no raising of hands), but your class may have developed its own particular customs.
- End by asking the students what they would do to make a visiting student feel welcome in their Touchpebbles class.

Total: 40 minutes

Worksheet 28: The Spider and the Turtle

INDIVIDUAL WORK, PART 1

1. Every family has its own customs, or ways of doing things that stay the same, that guests have to get used to. We notice our customs the most at holidays like Thanksgiving when we eat special foods and do special things together. Pick your favorite holiday and think of some of the special things your family does on that holiday. The questions below will help you with your answer. You can write down answers if you wish.

   a) What holiday is your favorite?

   b) If you get to eat special foods, which do you like best?

   c) Do you do any special activities together? What is one?

   d) What is one thing your family always tries to do together on that holiday?

SMALL GROUP WORK

Take turns sharing the special things your families do for your favorite holidays. Be sure to listen carefully to one another, and compare your answers.

INDIVIDUAL WORK, PART 2

2. What are the customs (the things you all do successfully) in your Touchpebbles class? Mark the boxes with a "✔."

❑ Never raise hands

❑ Don't interrupt people when we want to talk

❑ Listen with respect

❑ Help others get into the discussion

❑ Laugh when someone says something silly

(You write down one more)_____

Lesson 28: The Spider and the Turtle

The Spider and the Turtle
A Tale of the Ashanti People of Africa
(STUDENT VOLUME, PAGE 65)

It was nearly dark when the turtle found a clearing in the woods and rested. There was a wonderful smell of cooked fish and fresh fruit. He followed the smell and found the spider about to eat his dinner. The spider was unhappy to see the turtle because he didn't want to share his food. However, spiders have a law that says they must never refuse food to a stranger. So he invited the turtle in, and the tired turtle felt happy about his good luck. Just as the turtle was about to put food in his mouth, the spider said in a stern voice, "Turtle, in my country we always wash before eating. Please go to the stream and wash your paws. I see dust on them from your trip." The turtle wished to be a good guest and did as he was told. But when he returned, the spider had already eaten half the food. As the turtle tried to pick up some fish, the spider jumped across the table. "You call that washed?" he said, pointing to some dirt on the turtle's paws. The turtle felt ashamed and went back to the stream one more time. When he finally returned clean and ready to eat, all the food was gone. The turtle was angry but said, "Thank you for your invitation. Some day you must come and visit me."

A few months later, the spider was out walking and hurt himself. For a few days, he couldn't move. When he was finally able to walk, he struggled down to the river. There he found the turtle, who said, "Spider, you look terrible." The spider replied, "Yes, I was hurt and haven't eaten in days." The turtle smiled and said, "Well, come to my house at the bottom of the river and I will feed you a wonderful meal." The turtle went deep down into the water to prepare the food and the spider tried to follow. But he couldn't get to the bottom because he was so light. So the clever spider put many pebbles in his coat pockets and tried again. This time he sank down to the turtle's house. There he saw the most wonderful food he had ever seen. Excited by his good luck, he sat down and the turtle handed him a full plate. But, just as he was about to take a bite, the turtle said, "Spider, in my country, we never wear a coat to dinner. Please take off your coat." Very slowly the spider removed his coat. As he did, he began to rise in the water away from the table. Without the pebbles, he floated up to the surface as he watched all that wonderful food being eaten up by the turtle.

The moral of the story is that when you try to trick someone for selfish reasons, there is always someone trickier than you.

Lesson 29

A Map of Iceland
from the cover of Touchpebbles Volume A

PURPOSE
In discussions and in life, people must make decisions, such as whether to talk, remain silent, or ask questions. Today's lesson deals with making decisions and examining the results.

Students will:
- Analyze an ancient map and try to determine the mapmaker's intentions.
- Decide which elements to include in a map that they will create in class.

INTRODUCTION
One of the crucial skills emerging from participation in Touchpebbles is decision-making, about both what students say and what they do. Your students have now had a great deal of experience in discussing topics, working in small groups, and completing the worksheets to choose approaches, ideas, or strategies. Now, near the end of the volume, it is appropriate to make the topic of decision-making explicit. In this lesson, students will explore decision-making by considering how to make a map and how to read it.

Making a map involves making very clear choices. First, what is the purpose of the map? Suppose we consider a map of the United States without Alaska and Hawaii. Not every feature can be given equal value. Some features will be stressed, some played down, and many completely ignored. If the purpose of the map is to reveal political differences, it will outline the state borders, the county lines, or the voting districts. If the map's function to show topographical differences, it may ignore the states and counties to stress contour lines. A map used to navigate a river will be radically different from a map used to navigate a city. Even the outline

Lesson 29: A Map of Iceland

of the country, state, or county will change depending on whether one wants to represent the road system (in which case the outline might be schematized as simple straight lines at angles), or whether one wishes to have the proportional size of each state represent the differences in population. Using a map also requires learning how to read it and recognizing the perspective from which the map is drawn.

LESSON SUMMARY

The text for this lesson is the cover map of *Touchpebbles Volume A*. It is an early map of Iceland, and students will spend the first minutes of the class "reading" it with a great deal of help from you. With the whole class sitting in the usual circle, ask the students to try to identify what seems important to the person who drew this map. Have the students look at the features. Which is the most mountainous part of the country? Where are Iceland's live volcanoes? Where might the farming be good? You might note that there are no trees in the country, but valuable tree logs drift in on the eastern coast. Where are the important churches and monasteries, which are marked with a †? If the students landed in Iceland and had no way of leaving, where might they settle? Why?

For your information, the map presents other interesting features. Mountains are signified by round elevations (even though the actual mountains are jagged) and the word "Jokul." Only major mountains are marked. Hekla the volcano is depicted emitting fire and smoke as well as rocks. It was often the first thing sailors could see because they approached from the southeast. Various pictures of animals show where good pasturing or hunting could be found. Although hard to see, small birds perch on cliffs below Hekla. They are hawks and falcons, valuable as hunters and for the medieval sport of falconry. The various sea creatures, including whales and good fish to eat, are part fanciful and part realistic. The dotted line in the middle divides two church dioceses. Note that the map does not depict trails or roads. Finally, in the northeast, the mapmaker depicts ice floes on which are polar bears, animals that are very dangerous to unwary hunters. If possible, you may want to show the students pictures of Iceland or a modern map. The people who discovered Iceland gave it that name to discourage settlers because they considered it a very good place to live.

The worksheet for this lesson asks the students to draw a map to help a friend go the last few blocks or the final distance to visit them at their house. But first the students will complete a checklist to decide what features to represent. The students will choose landmarks that their friend should look for, such as a church, a school, or other houses. The students should also consider how their house is most easily recognized, for example, by its color, distinctive features, street number, or vegetation in front. Also, the students should take into account how their friend will get there (by car, on foot, or by bike) and indicate the best routes for each for each means of travel (they may be the same or different).The students should also consider potential problems or dangers, such as a fierce dog nearby, a bad hole in the street, and so forth. After they decide on the features, the students should then draw a map that incorporates these features. You will probably need to give them a great deal of guidance for this exercise.

When the students have completed all these tasks, ask them to pair off. In these pairs, the students should try to read each other's maps. Finally, after bringing the whole class together again in a circle, turn the discussion to any difficulties the students encountered in creating and reading the maps. In particular, you should have them compare reading a map with reading a painting, a story, and a poem.

Possible Questions to Raise

Discussion, Part 1
- What do you think was most important to the person who drew the map?
- Which is the most mountainous part of the country?
- Where on the map do you think farming is good?
- Where on the map would you like to live?

Discussion, Part 2
- Was it difficult to draw a map? Why?
- How did you decide what to include in your map?
- Is reading a map like reading a book, poem, or painting?

Lesson 29: A Map of Iceland

LESSON PLAN 29

Activity	Time
1. ARRANGE CLASSROOM	1 min.
2. MAP	2 min.

- Tell the students that the first part of today's lesson is to look at the map on the cover of *Touchpebbles Volume A*.
- Explain that it is a map of Iceland drawn hundreds of years ago. You may wish to have them locate Iceland on a globe so that they can see how close it is to the North Pole.

3. DISCUSSION, PART 1 .... 5 min.
- Ask them to pick out details; help them as you see fit.

4. INDIVIDUAL WORK .... 15 min.
- Pass out the worksheet and ask the students to complete the Individual Work and draw their own map.
- Explain the connection between the worksheet questions and their drawing of the map.

5. PAIR WORK .... 7 min.
- Pair off the students (form a group of three, if necessary) and have them read each other's maps.

6. DISCUSSION, PART 2 .... 10 min.
- Reconvene the large group and discuss what made the exercise difficult. The students may also discuss the cover map again.

Total: 40 minutes

Worksheet 29: A Map of Iceland

INDIVIDUAL WORK

1. A friend is coming to see you at your house but has never been there before. You want your friend to have a map so he or she does not get lost. Check the features below that you think your map should include to get your friend safely to your house. For each question below, you can check one or more boxes.

   a) How will your friend know it's your house?
      - ❏ color
      - ❏ street number can be seen
      - ❏ near other houses or buildings
      - ❏ unusual parts of the house such as big driveway, porch, or a large garage with basketball backboard on it
      - ❏ trees or bushes in front

   b) How will your friend get there?
      - ❏ car, so roads need to be drawn
      - ❏ on foot, so walking route needs to be shown
      - ❏ bike, so bike path needs to be shown

   c) Are there any very big buildings, hills, or rivers nearby that your friend will see and know that he or she is close to your house?
      - ❏ churches or schools or large stores
      - ❏ hills, river, lake, or some other natural feature

   d) Is there anything your friend should be careful about?
      - ❏ big dogs or other animals
      - ❏ broken sidewalks or holes in the streets
      - ❏ dangerous area

2. On the back of this paper, draw a map of the area close to your house, about the last two blocks, and put the things you checked in question 1 on your map.

PAIR WORK

Take your partner's map and try to read it as best you can. Point out things that seem unclear to you and ask your partner questions about why he or she drew his or her map that way.

Lesson

The Histories
by Herodotus

PURPOSE

How we recognize and judge others' points of view and customs has been an ongoing theme throughout your Touchpebbles classes. Lesson 30 will deal directly with this theme by examining how we come to understand a perspective outside our own.

Students will:
- Read a text about the ancient customs of the Persian culture and compare them to their own.
- Imagine how people who have a different culture might react to students' ideas and customs.
- Discuss how the customs of, and students' behaviors in, their Touchpebbles class have changed since the beginning of the year.

INTRODUCTION

This last class of *Touchpebbles Volume A* is an appropriate time to review the kinds of skills you and your students have practiced in Touchpebbles Discussions. One skill is sensitivity to the fact that different people view themselves, the world, and others from different points of view. Two subsequent skills are necessary: to learn to grasp or understand a different point of view, and then to judge it.

Grasping or understanding a point of view first involves trying to imagine the circumstances that would make it plausible for people to have that viewpoint. Does their behavior reflect a sensible response to their particular individual or national circumstances? Although their behavior or customs may differ from ours, their processes of thinking or reasoning might be quite recognizable to us. This recognition does not imply, however, that their response is correct or justified, only that it is not plainly absurd. To grasp something that initially seems strange to us involves trying to imagine the circumstances that would tempt us to act or think similarly.

Lesson 30: The Histories

The second step in grasping another point of view is to try to think from within that point of view. Such perspective can often be achieved by trying to look at ourselves from the point of view of other people. We can ask ourselves what actions or opinions of ours would appear strange or peculiar to the people we are trying to understand. This enables us to notice aspects of ourselves that perhaps we had never noticed before, maybe ones that are so familiar that we never notice them.

This second step enables us to contrast our viewpoint with that of others, and then make a judgment. This week's lesson encourages students to practice making comparisons that will allow them to make a sound judgment about another point of view.

Lesson Summary

The text by Herodotus describes some of the customs of the ancient Persians. These customs were different from the customs of Herodotus' own people, the Greeks of the fifth century B.C., and are quite different from our customs today. Herodotus describes some of the customs without making any judgment. Others, such as the custom that a father does not see his son during the first five years of the child's life, he judges favorably. In considering this text, the students should discuss whether they can supply good reasons for the Persian customs and whether they can approve of the last two customs listed on the worksheet (Persian boys under five years old don't see their fathers, and Persian kings cannot execute anyone for just one crime).

The worksheet, which should be done after reading the text, will help the students make their opinions explicit. It asks them to check the Persian customs that they think make sense. In addition, it also lists some American customs and asks for students' opinions on how the Persians would react to them. For example, we teach boys and girls in the same way. Do the students think the Persians would like what we do? Also, Americans think that children should be raised by both parents from birth. The Persians would probably not like that.

Since this is the last meeting for this volume, it would be useful during the last ten minutes of class to encourage the students to reflect on how they have changed as a group throughout previous classes. Do their present customs, or how they act in the Touchpebbles class, differ from the way they behaved at the start of the year?

Possible Questions to Raise

- Which of your customs do you think the ancient Persians would like the most? Why?
- Which custom would be the hardest for you to follow in Persia? Why?
- Do you think the Persians should teach both boys and girls like we do?
- Is there a custom of yours that you think would seem strange to other people?

Lesson 30: The Histories

LESSON PLAN 30

Activity   Time

1. **ARRANGE CLASSROOM** .... 1 min.
2. **TEXT** .... 2 min.
   - Read the text aloud while students read along silently.

3. **INDIVIDUAL WORK** .... 7 min.
   - Pass out the worksheet and have the students check answers to both questions.
4. **SMALL GROUP WORK** .... 10 min.
   - Divide the class into groups of four or five students.
   - Have them share answers to questions 1 and 2 in the Individual Work and come to a consensus on what customs the ancient Persians would like. The students might disagree over 2c, because nothing in the text explicitly says what the Persians thought about freedom.
5. **DISCUSSION** .... 20 min.
   - Reconvene the large circle and have the small groups report on their answers to question 2. Allow for general discussion on these answers. Reserve the last ten minutes of class to discuss whether the customs or habits the students now have in Touchpebbles Discussions are different from those they had at the beginning of the Touchpebbles program.

Total: 40 minutes

TOUCHPEBBLES VOLUME A

Lesson 30: The Histories

The Histories
by Herodotus
(STUDENT VOLUME, PAGE 69)

The customs of the Persians are very different from ours. The Persians have no pictures of the gods, no special temples or churches, and no altars. They think that those people who do have such things are foolish because the Persians believe God is everywhere. When they wish to pray, they climb to the highest mountain tops. A person who goes to worship God never says a prayer for himself alone. He must also pray for the health and success of the ruler, and then for the good fortune of the entire people.

They give the greatest respect to the country nearest to them. Those who live a little farther away are honored somewhat less. Those who live farthest away are considered worthless. Yet no one uses ideas from other peoples' customs as much as the Persians do. Whenever they hear about something new in another country, they right away do the same themselves.

Next to strength and bravery in battle, the greatest respect is paid to a man because he has fathered many sons. From the ages of five to twenty, a boy is carefully taught only three things: to ride, to shoot an arrow from a bow, and to speak the truth. Until a boy is five, he does not ever see his father. This is so the father will not be sad if the boy dies. To my mind, this is a wise rule and so is the next difference between them and us.

The ruler cannot put anyone to death for only a single fault or crime, no matter what it is. In every such case, the good a person did is compared with the bad. If the bad is greater than the good, then the person is punished. Persians also hold that it is against the law to talk about anything that is unlawful to do. The worst thing in the world, they think, is to tell a lie. The second worst thing is to owe someone money because a person who owes money must tell lies.

Worksheet 30: The Histories

INDIVIDUAL WORK

1. Which of the Persian customs make sense to you?

    a) Persians have no churches.
    ❏ Makes sense   ❏ Doesn't make sense

    b) Persians pray on mountain tops.
    ❏ Makes sense   ❏ Doesn't make sense

    c) Persians don't respect nations far away from them.
    ❏ Makes sense   ❏ Doesn't make sense

    d) Persians most respect a man who has many sons.
    ❏ Makes sense   ❏ Doesn't make sense

    e) Persian boys only learn to ride, shoot an arrow, and tell the truth.
    ❏ Makes sense   ❏ Doesn't make sense

    f) Persian boys under five years old don't see their father.
    ❏ Makes sense   ❏ Doesn't make sense

    g. Persian kings cannot execute anyone for just one crime.
    ❏ Makes sense   ❏ Doesn't make sense

2. Below are some of our nation's customs. Which ones would the Persians like?

    a) We teach boys and girls the same things.
    ❏ Persians would like   ❏ Persians don't like

    b) People can pray however they wish.
    ❏ Persians would like   ❏ Persians don't like

    c) We most respect nations that are free like us.
    ❏ Persians would like   ❏ Persians don't like

d) We tend to respect people who help others.
   ❏ Persians would like   ❏ Persians don't like

e) We don't mind what people say; what they do matters most.
   ❏ Persians would like   ❏ Persians don't like

f) We let people owe money.
   ❏ Persians would like   ❏ Persians don't like

g) Children are raised by both parents from birth.
   ❏ Persians would like   ❏ Persians don't like

SMALL GROUP WORK

Share your answers to questions 1 and 2 in the Individual Work and agree on what customs the Persians would like.

APPENDIX A

Guidelines for Opening Questions

1. Your opening question should be short so that it is easy for students to understand and to remember.

2. Your opening question should start the discussion. However, it should not be the only question or subject about which the class will talk.

3. Your question should touch on something in the reading but does not have to be exclusively about the reading.

4. When thinking about an opening question, ask yourself what in the reading you think would interest others in the class.

APPENDIX B

Observation Sheet

Class: _____

Lesson: _____

GROUP EVALUATION

"1" indicates dynamic does not exist, and "10" indicates dynamic is extremely present.

1. Dominance by one or a few individuals.
   1   2   3   4   5   6   7   8   9   10

2. Balanced participation by group members.
   1   2   3   4   5   6   7   8   9   10

3. Cooperative exploration of a topic.
   1   2   3   4   5   6   7   8   9   10

4. Disagreements for the mere sake of disagreement.
   1   2   3   4   5   6   7   8   9   10

5. Engagement level by the group (listening attentively and speaking both count).
   1   2   3   4   5   6   7   8   9   10

6. Participation helped and encouraged among the participants.
   1   2   3   4   5   6   7   8   9   10

7. Respect shown to members of the group.
   1   2   3   4   5   6   7   8   9   10

8. Desire by group members to hear different perspectives.
   1   2   3   4   5   6   7   8   9   10

9. Assistance given to one another to clarify and explore a point.
   1   2   3   4   5   6   7   8   9   10

10. Ownership of the process by the group.
    1   2   3   4   5   6   7   8   9   10

Leader Evaluation

1. Asks helpful questions.
       1   2   3   4   5   6   7   8   9   10

2. Lets students be independent.
       1   2   3   4   5   6   7   8   9   10

3. Aware of quieter students and including everyone in the group.
       1   2   3   4   5   6   7   8   9   10

4. comfortable, confident.
       1   2   3   4   5   6   7   8   9   10

5. Includes and allows discussion about both experiences and text.
       1   2   3   4   5   6   7   8   9   10

6. Attempts to get participants to listen and respond to one another.
       1   2   3   4   5   6   7   8   9   10

APPENDIX C

The Orientation Class Revisited

"1" indicates dynamic does not exist, and "10" indicates dynamic is extremely present.

1. How well do you think the class has been reading the Touchstones Texts? (ground rule 1)

    1   2   3   4   5   6   7   8   9   10

2. How well do you think the class has been listening to each other and not interrupting? (Ground Rule 2)

    1   2   3   4   5   6   7   8   9   10

3. Overall, do you think students speak clearly in the discussion? (ground rule 3)

    1   2   3   4   5   6   7   8   9   10

4. Overall, do you think students are respectful toward one another during discussions? (ground rule 4)

    1   2   3   4   5   6   7   8   9   10

5. Would you say that the discussions involve everyone in the classroom?
    Please explain your answer.

6. Are the discussions usually about students' personal experiences and opinions as well as about the readings?

7. Which ground rule do you need to keep in mind when participating in discussions?

APPENDIX D

1. Make a mark below for each time that someone speaks.

2. How many students are in the discussion today?

3. How many spoke?

4. Of the students who did not speak, did they look interested? How could you tell?

5. Of the students who did speak, did they usually speak to everyone in the whole group, to the teacher, or to the same students? How could you tell?

6. How can the group improve in the future?

7. Because you were an observer and were not part of the discussion, do you think the discussion would have gone any differently if you had not been there? If so, how?

APPENDIX E

Directions: Brainstorm in small groups what to do in the given situations. Write a brief response in the space underneath each scenario.

What do you do or say during a discussion when—

1. you don't understand what someone is saying?

2. you think what someone is saying doesn't make much sense?

3. you agree with what someone is saying, but you want to add something?

4. you weren't paying attention, but now want to know what's happening in the discussion?

5. you disagree with someone?

6. someone has been talking a long time?

7. you notice someone keeps getting cut off or interrupted?

8. you can't hear the speaker because he or she is speaking too softly?

9. you can't hear the speaker because other students are talking or making noise?

10. other students continue to cut you off?

11. someone misunderstands what you just said?

APPENDIX F

1. Rate your participation in the Touchstones classes this year. Circle your choice, with "1" being very poor and "10" being excellent.

    1   2   3   4   5   6   7   8   9   10

2. Why did you rate yourself that way?

3. What could you do to improve your participation?

4. What could you do to improve the discussion?

5. What explanation would you choose to explain why you have not always been as active a participant as you could be?

    a) The texts are usually too difficult.
    b) Too many people talk at once.
    c) I have not been sure what I could say that would help the discussion.
    d) I prefer to listen.
    e) I have a difficult time expressing what I want to say.
    f) I have not thought about what I could do differently before this activity.
    g) Other _____.

6. Answer the following questions after the discussion: How was your participation today? Were you able to try new strategies? How or why not?

Lesson 5, Hound and Hunter (1892)

Lesson 15, Portrait of a Clergyman (1516)

Marchesa Brigida Spinola Doria (1606)

Waves at Matsushima (17th Century)

Lesson 10, The Much Resounding Sea (1884)